RECORDED VERSIONS GUITAR

AUTHENTIC TRANSCRIPTIONS
WITH NOTES AND TABLATURE

MAROON 5
E.P.L. - HIG

SONGS**ABOUT**JANE

D0521479

CONTENTS

Music transcriptions by Jeff Jacobson and David Stocker

ISBN 0-634-06876-8

HAL•LEONARD®
CORPORATION
7777 W. BLUEMOUND RD. P.O. BOX 13819 MILWAUKEE, WI 53213

Visit Hal Leonard Online at
www.halleonard.com

Harder to Breathe

Words and Music by Adam Levine and Jesse Carmichael

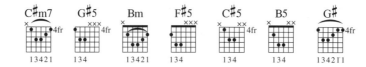

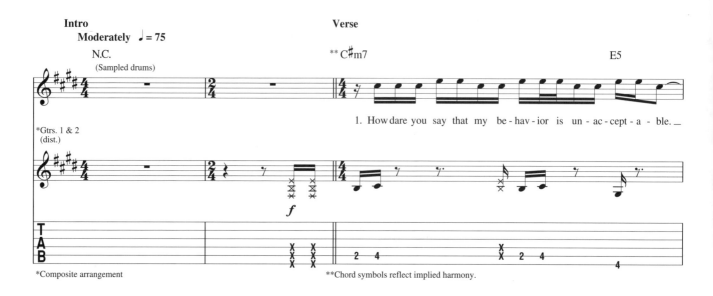

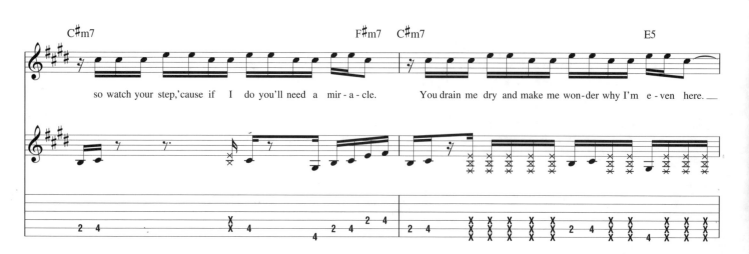

3

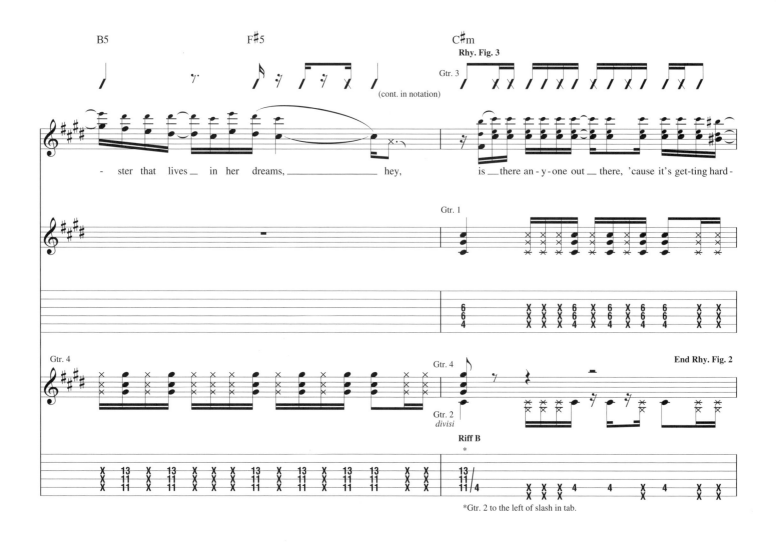

-ster that lives __ in her dreams, _____ hey,   is __ there an - y-one out __ there, 'cause it's get-ting hard-

*Gtr. 2 to the left of slash in tab.

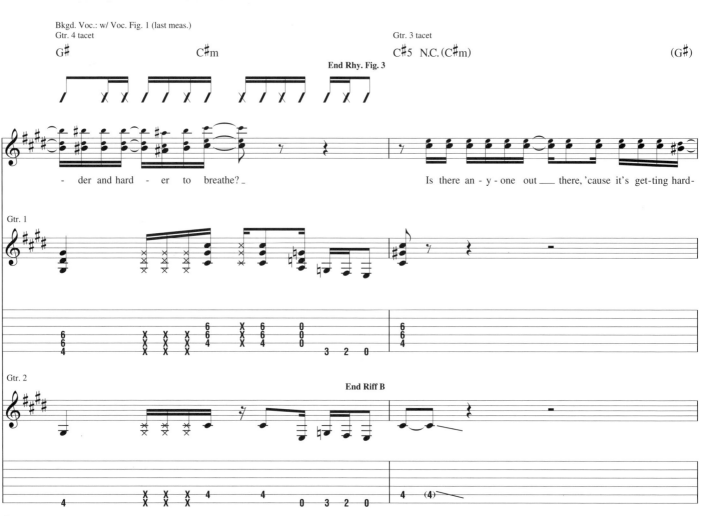

-der and hard - er to breathe? _   Is there an - y - one out __ there, 'cause it's get-ting hard-

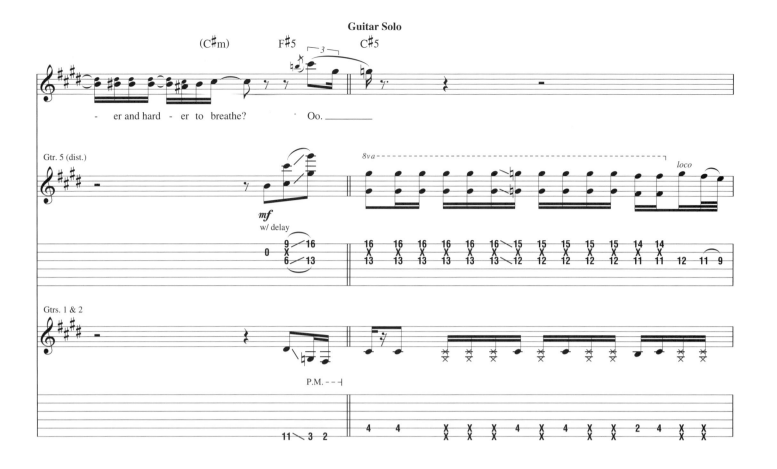

- er and hard - er to breathe? Oo. _____

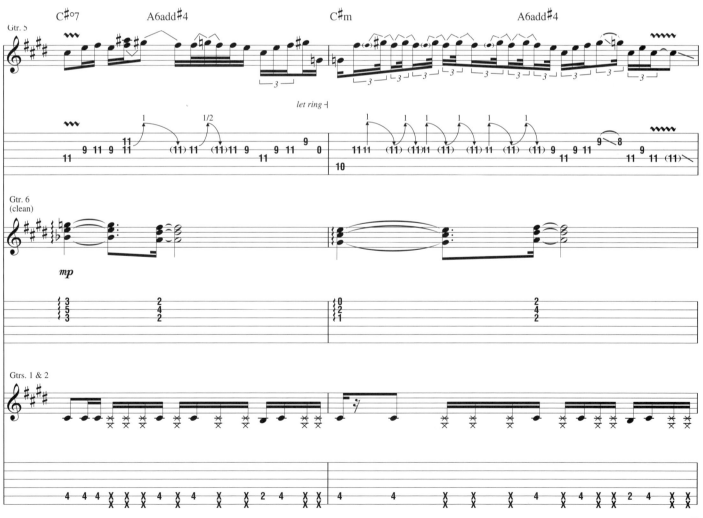

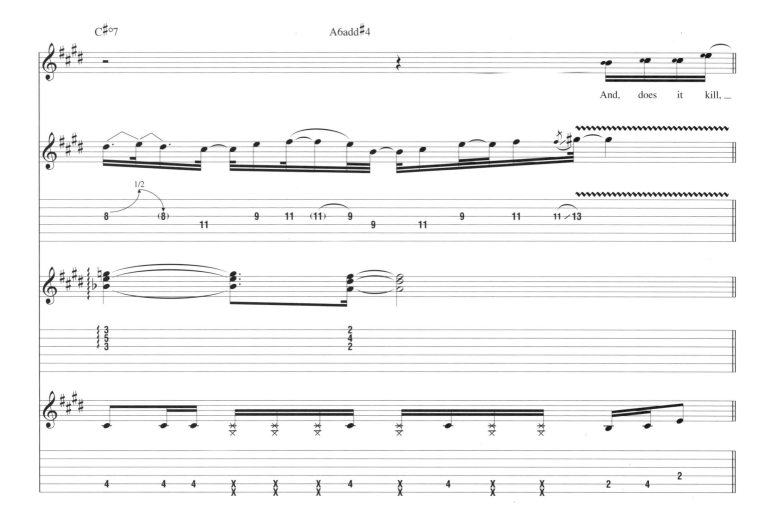

And, does it kill, ___

Bridge

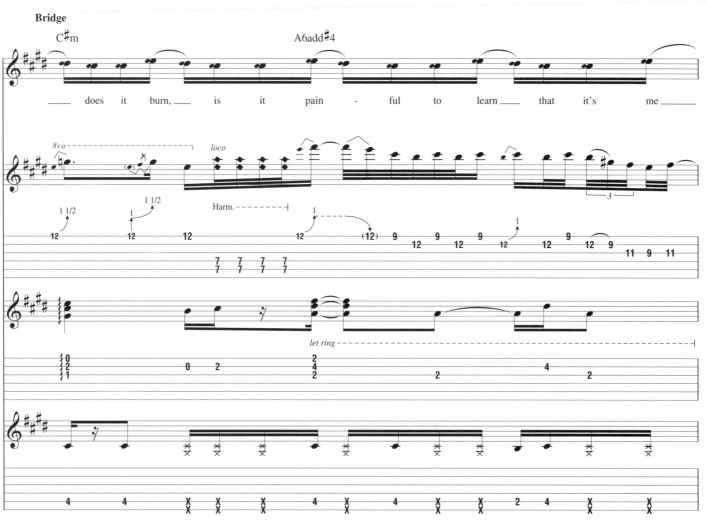

___ does it burn, ___ is it pain - ful to learn ___ that it's me ___

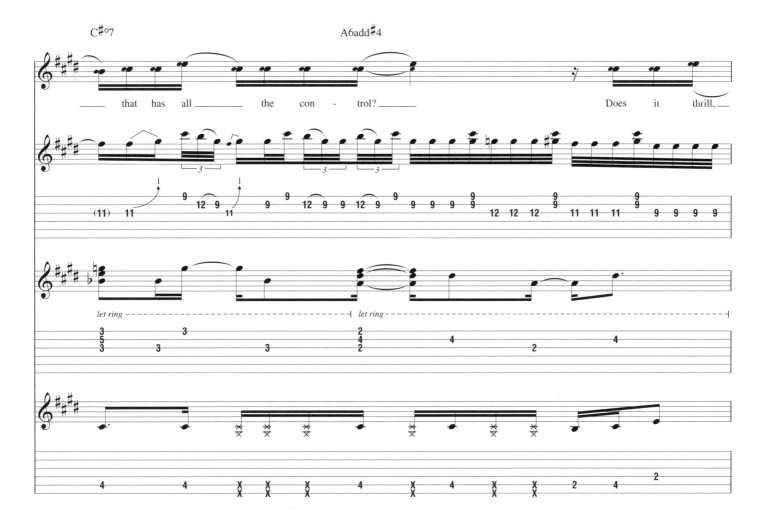

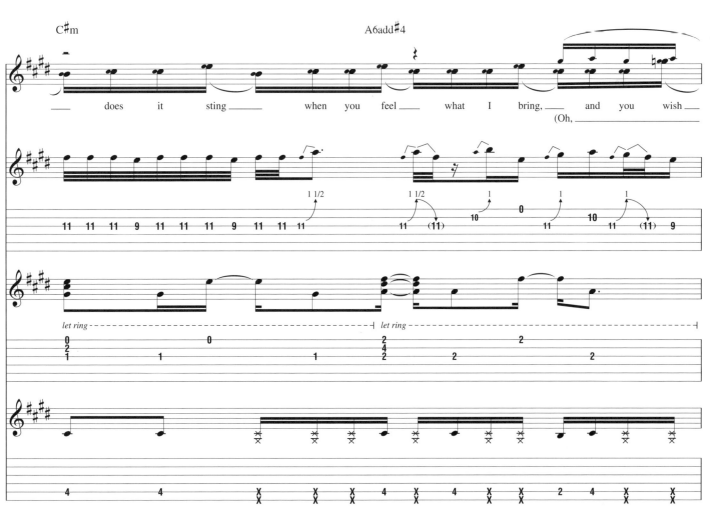

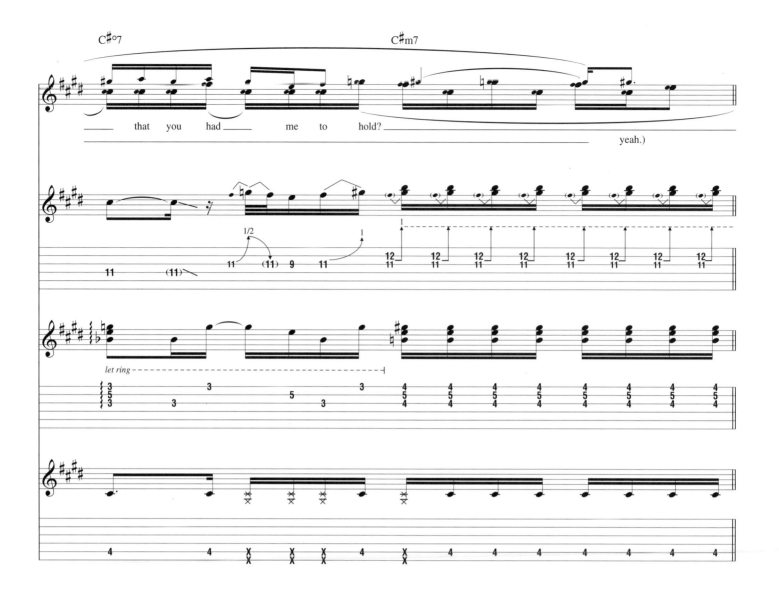

that you had ____ me to hold? _____

(yeah.)

let ring- - - - - - - - - - - - - - - - - - - -

Chorus

Gtrs. 1 & 2: w/ Riff A
Gtrs. 3 & 4: w/ Rhy. Figs. 1 & 2

Bkgd. Voc.: w/ Voc. Fig. 1
Gtrs. 5 & 6 tacet

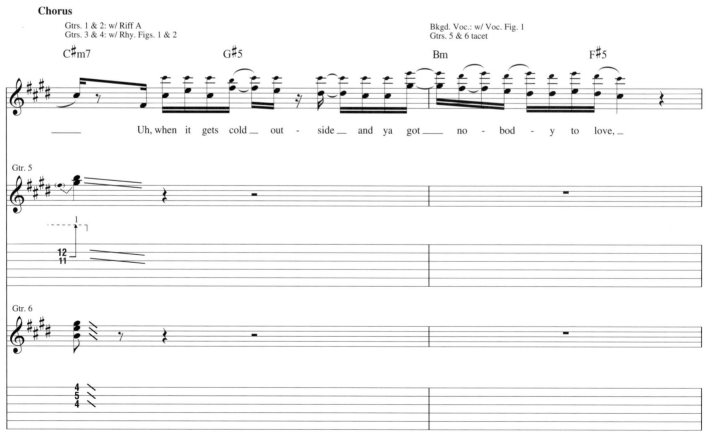

C#m7   G#5   Bm   F#5

____ Uh, when it gets cold ____ out - side ____ and ya got ____ no - bod - y to love, ____

Gtr. 5

Gtr. 6

C#m7   G#5   Bm   F#5

you'll un-der-stand what I mean __ when I say __ there's no way __ we're gon - na give up. __

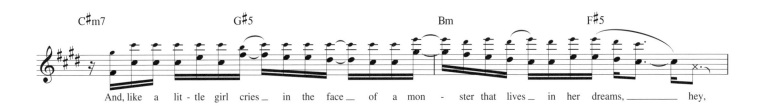

C#m7   G#5   Bm   F#5

And, like a lit-tle girl cries __ in the face __ of a mon - ster that lives __ in her dreams, _____ hey,

Gtr. 2: w/ Riff B
Gtr. 3: w/ Rhy. Fig. 3   Bkgd. Voc.: w/ Voc. Fig. 1 (last meas.)

C#m7   G#   C#m

is __ there an - y - one out __ there, 'cause it's get-ting hard - er and hard - er to breathe? _____

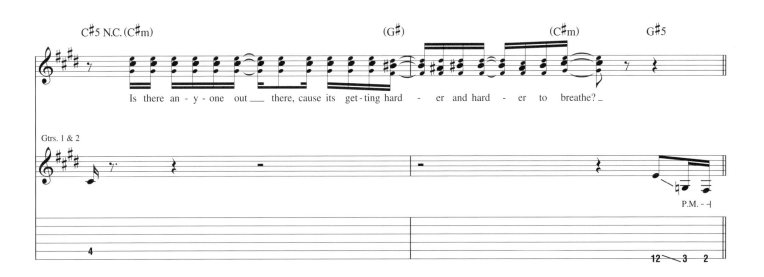

C#5 N.C. (C#m)   (G#)   (C#m)   G#5

Is there an - y - one out __ there, cause its get-ting hard - er and hard - er to breathe? _

Gtrs. 1 & 2

P.M. - ⌐

4   12 ⟍ 3   2

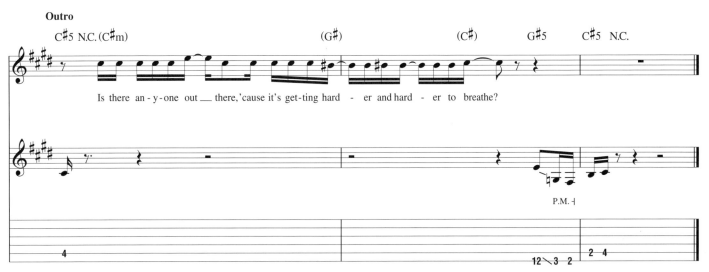

Outro

C#5 N.C. (C#m)   (G#)   (C#)   G#5   C#5 N.C.

Is there an - y - one out __ there, 'cause it's get-ting hard - er and hard - er to breathe?

P.M. ⌐

4   12 ⟍ 3   2   2   4

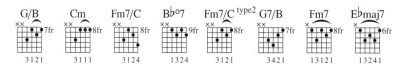

This Love

Words and Music by Adam Levine and Jesse Carmichael

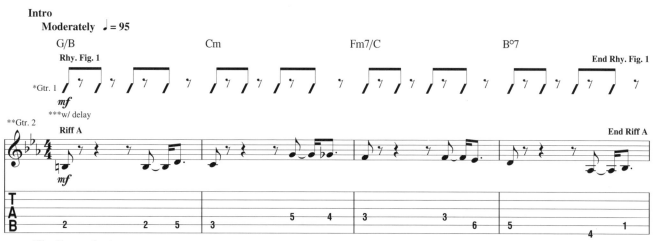

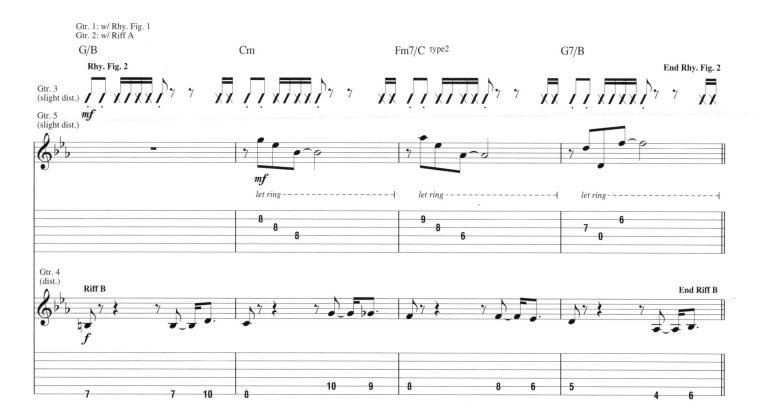

*Elec. Piano arr. for gtr.
**Piano arr. for gtr.
***Set for eighth-note regeneration w/ 1 repeat.

1. I was ___ so high, ___ I did ___ not rec-og-nize ___ the fire burn - ing in her eyes, ___ the cha-os that ___ con -trolled ___

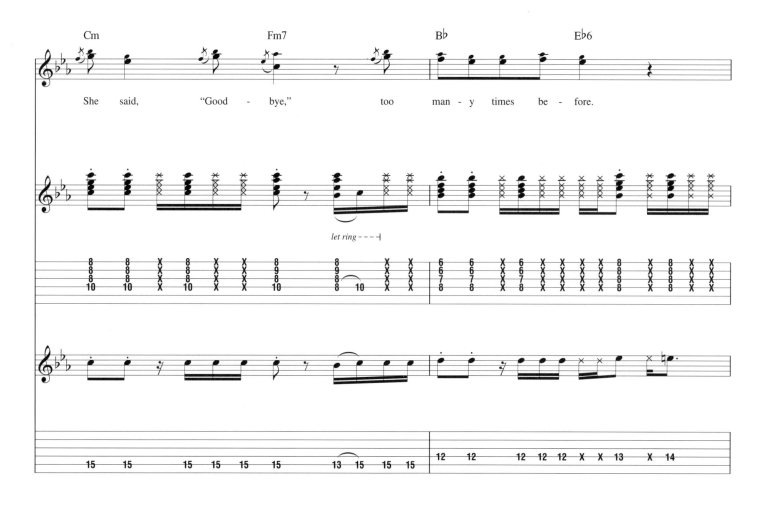

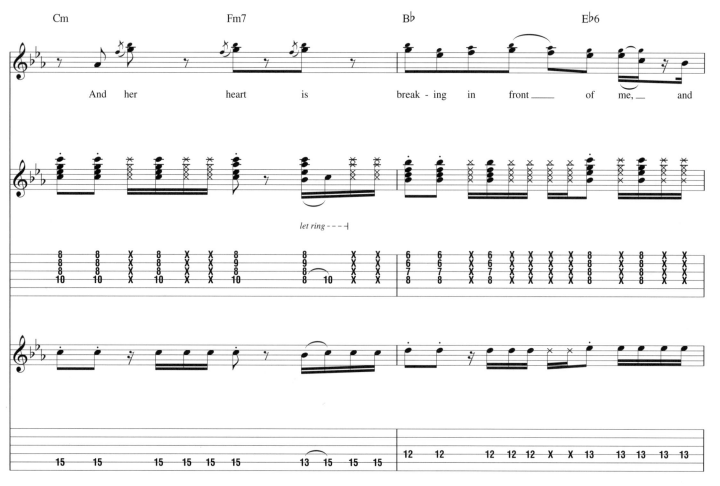

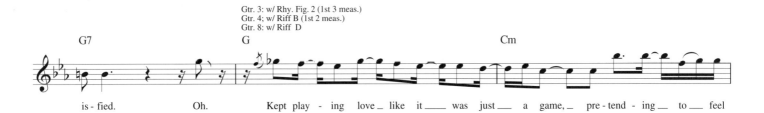

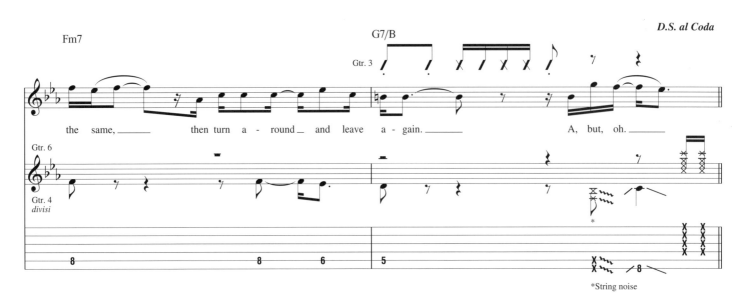

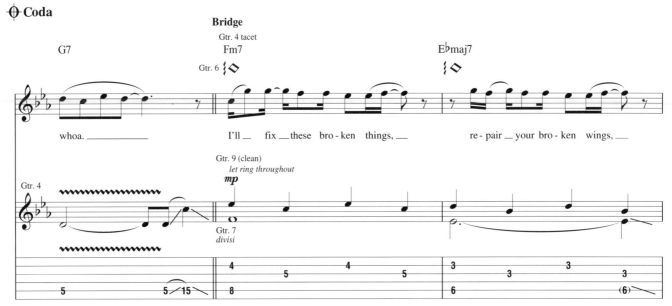

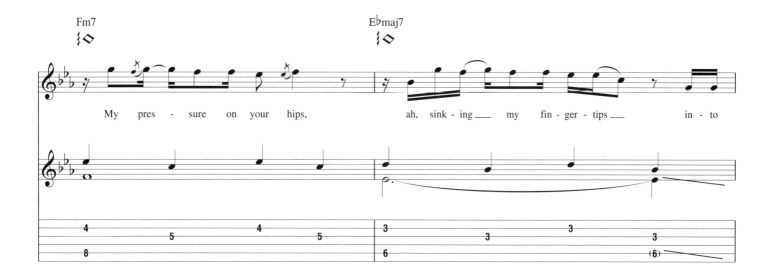

My pres - sure on your hips, ah, sink - ing my fin - ger - tips in - to

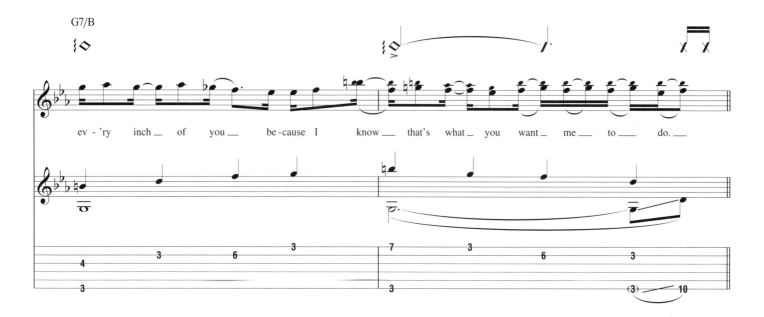

ev - 'ry inch of you be - cause I know that's what you want me to do.

Outro-Chorus
Gtr. 6: w/ Rhy. Fig. 3 (till fade)
Gtr. 7: w/ Riff C
Gtr. 9 tacet

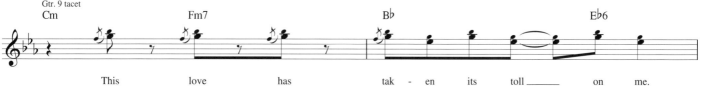

Cm | Fm7 | Bb | Eb6

This love has tak - en its toll on me.

Cm | Fm7 | Bb | Eb6 | Cm | Fm7

She said, "Good - bye," too man - y times be - fore. Her heart is

Bb | Eb6 | Cm | F

break - ing in front of me, and I have no choice 'cause

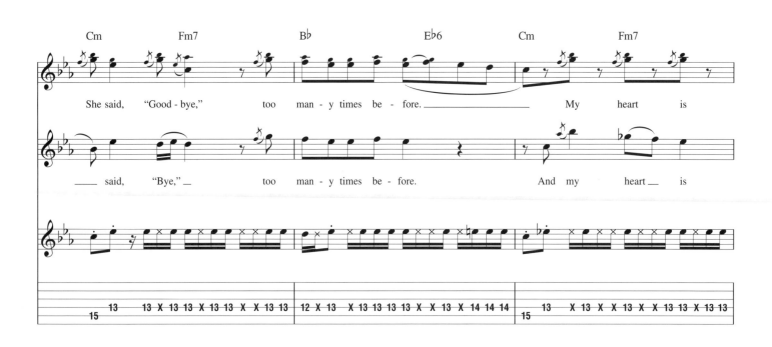

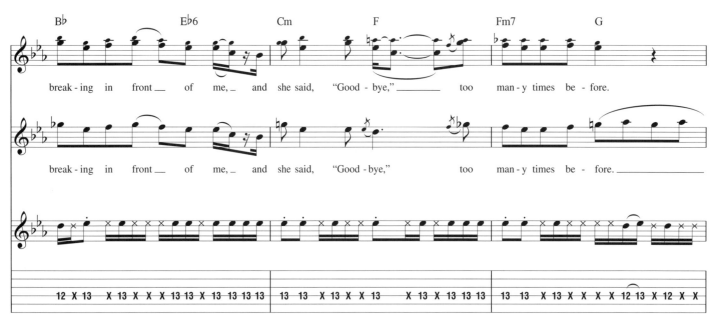

18

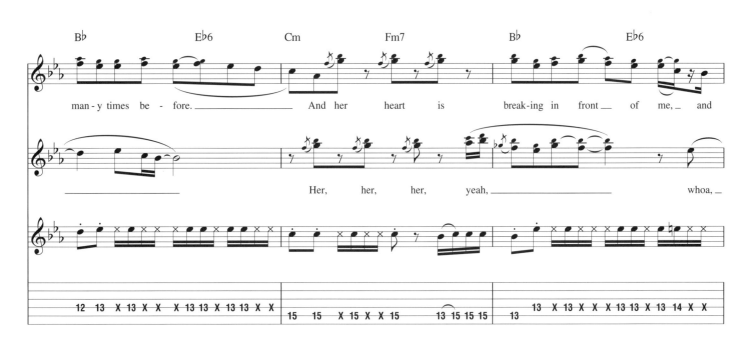

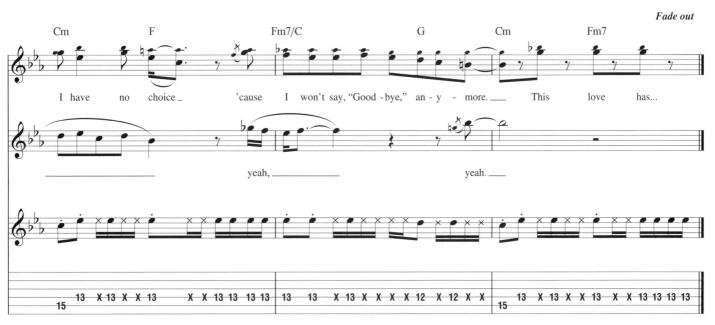

Shiver

Words and Music by Adam Levine and Jesse Carmichael

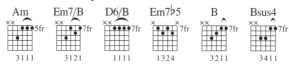

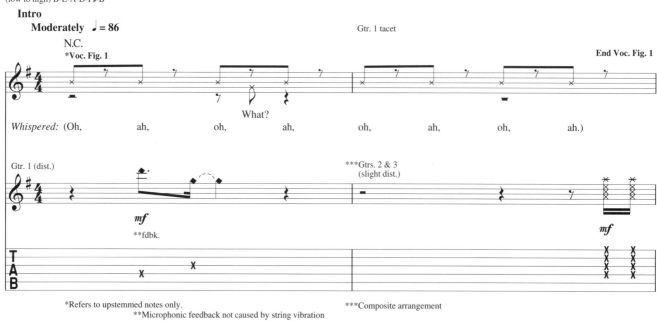

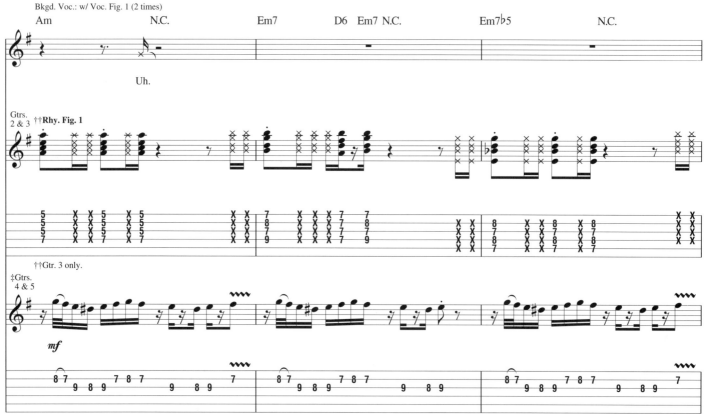

‡Gtr. 4: Elec. sitar arr. for gtr. Gtr. 5: w/ dist. & octaver. Set octaver for one octave below with equal mix of wet and dry signal.

Verse

Gtr. 3: w/ Rhy. Fig. 1
Gtrs. 4 & 5 tacet

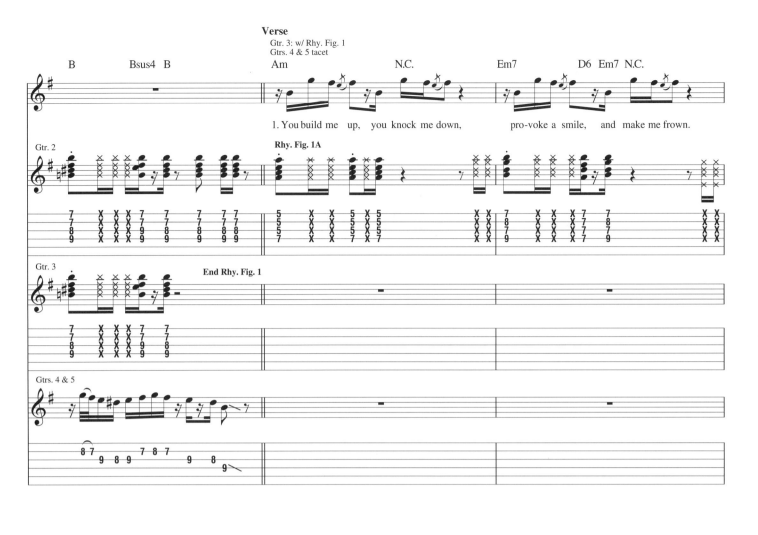

1. You build me up, you knock me down, pro-voke a smile, and make me frown.

You are the queen of run-a-round, you know it's __ true. __ You chew me up and spit me out,

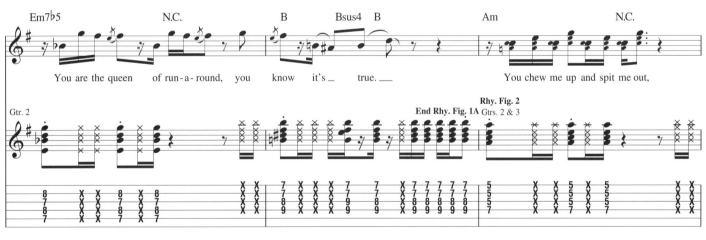

en-joy the taste I leave in your mouth. You look at me, I look at you, nei-ther of us know what to do. __

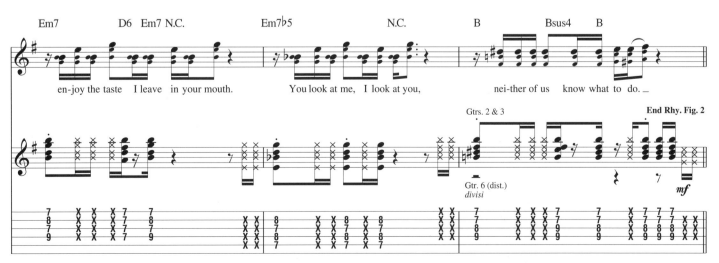

𝄋 **Chorus**

Gtrs. 2 & 3 tacet

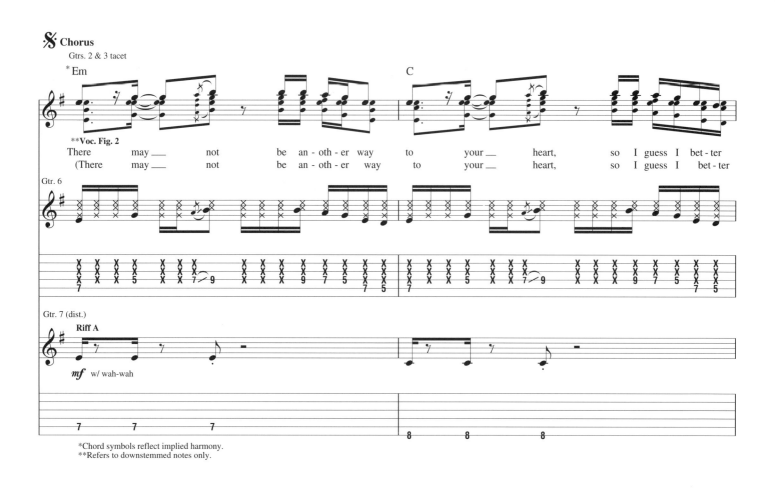

*Chord symbols reflect implied harmony.
**Refers to downstemmed notes only.

***Chord symbols in parentheses reflect chord names respective to tuned-down guitar. Symbols above represent actual sounding chords.

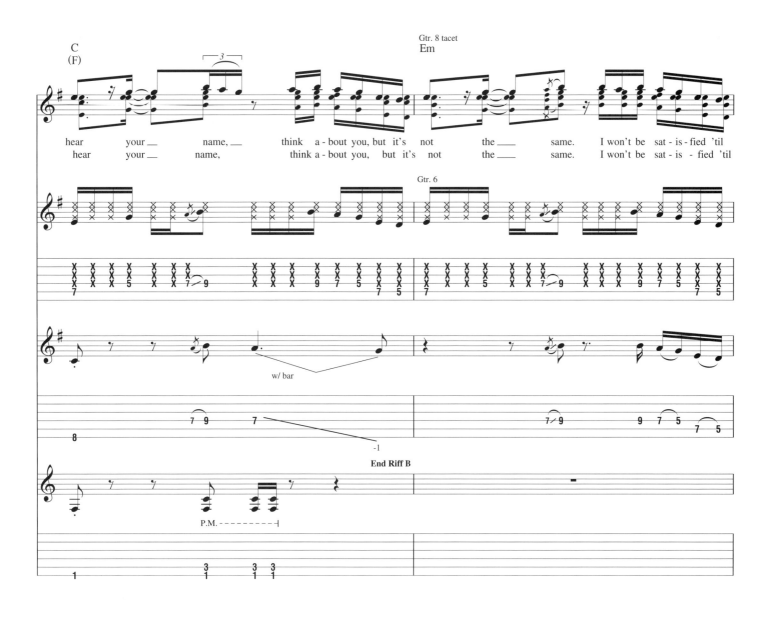

hear your __ name, __ think a - bout you, but it's not the __ same. I won't be sat - is - fied 'til
hear your __ name, think a - bout you, but it's not the __ same. I won't be sat - is - fied 'til

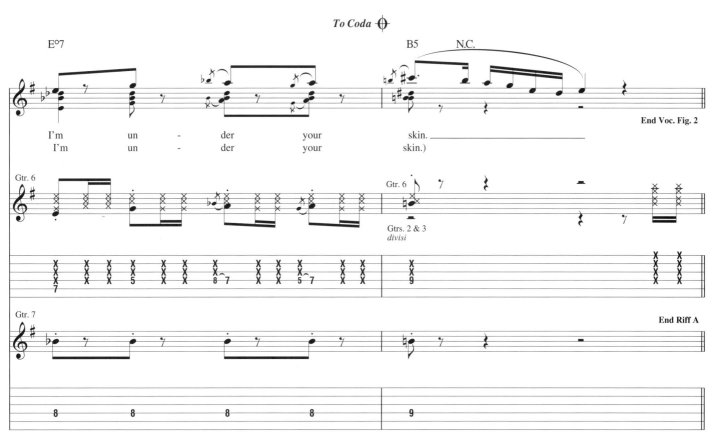

I'm un - der your skin. _____
I'm un - der your skin.)

Interlude

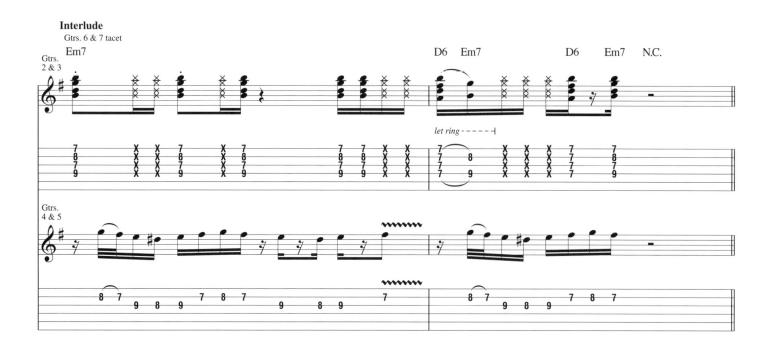

Verse

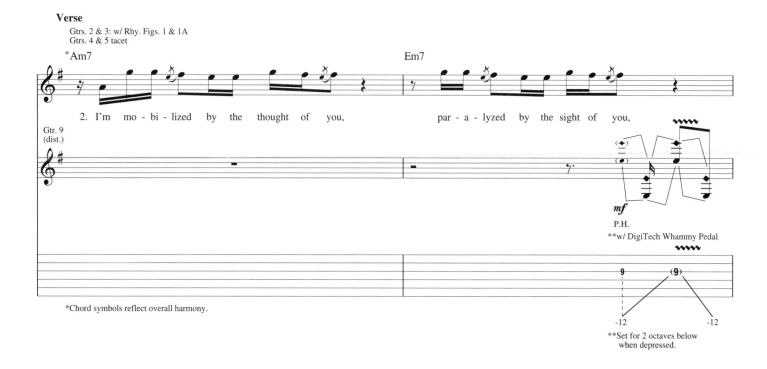

*Chord symbols reflect overall harmony.
**Set for 2 octaves below when depressed.

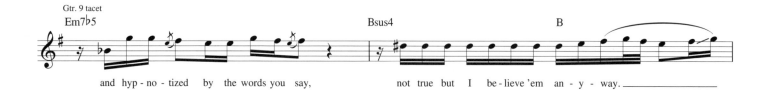

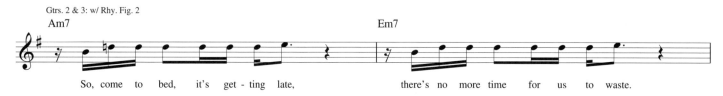

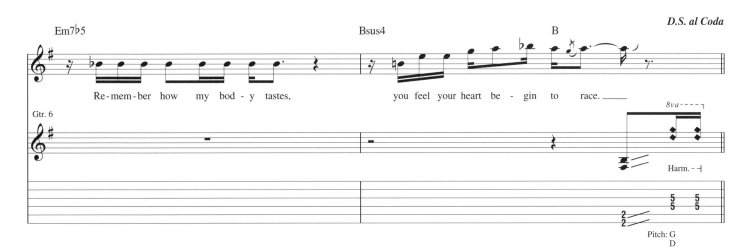

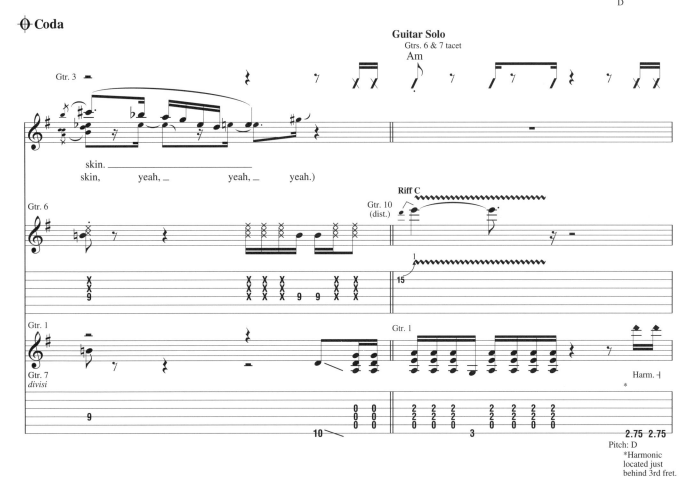

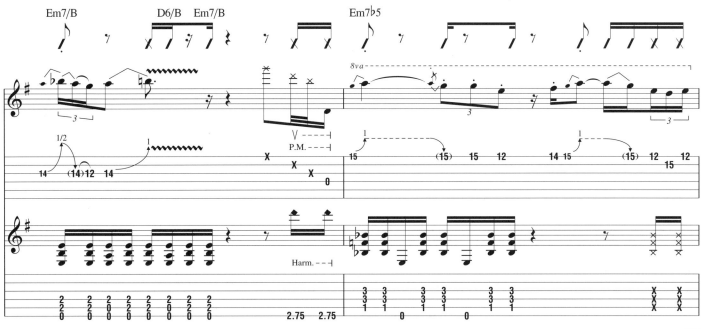

Outro-Chorus

Bkgd. Voc.: w/ Voc. Fig. 2 (2 times)
Gtrs. 1, 3 & 10 tacet
Gtr. 7: w/ Riff A (2 times)

Feel your heart be-gin to race. There may__ not be an-oth-er way

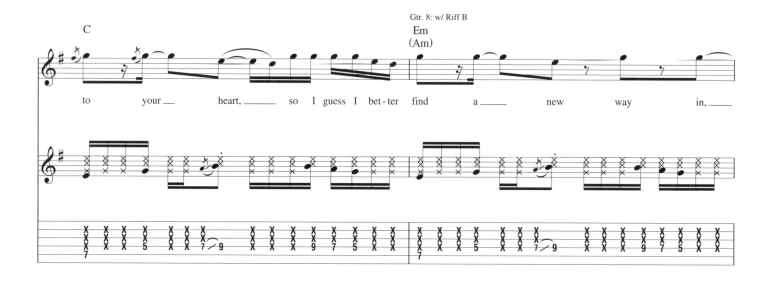

to your — heart, — so I guess I bet-ter find a — new way in, —

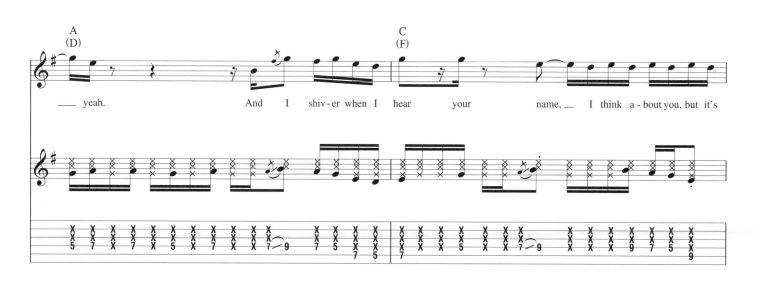

— yeah. And I shiv-er when I hear your name, — I think a-bout you, but it's

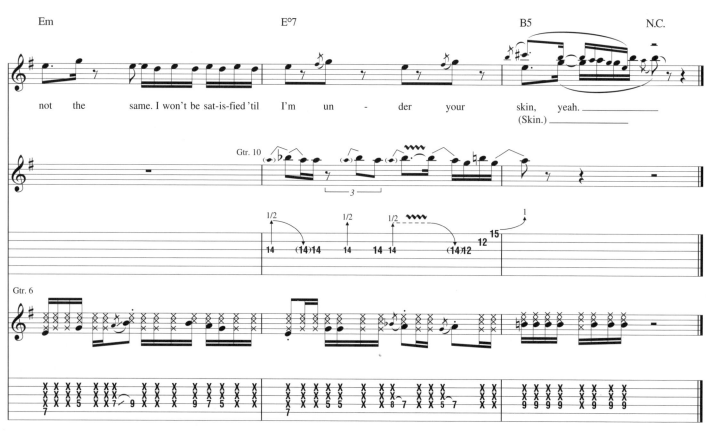

not the same. I won't be sat-is-fied 'til I'm un - der your skin, yeah. —
(Skin.) —

She Will Be Loved

Words and Music by Adam Levine and James Valentine

Look for the girl with the bro-ken smile, ___ ask her if she wants to stay a - while. And she will ___

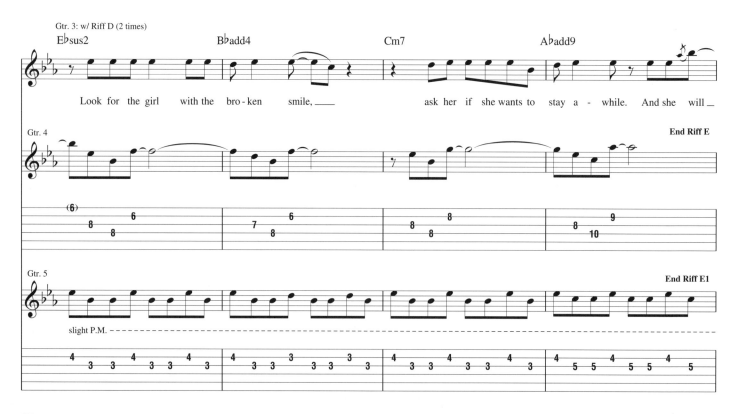

Chorus

Gtr. 3: w/ Riff D (3 3/4 times)
Gtr. 4 & 5: w/ Riffs E & E1

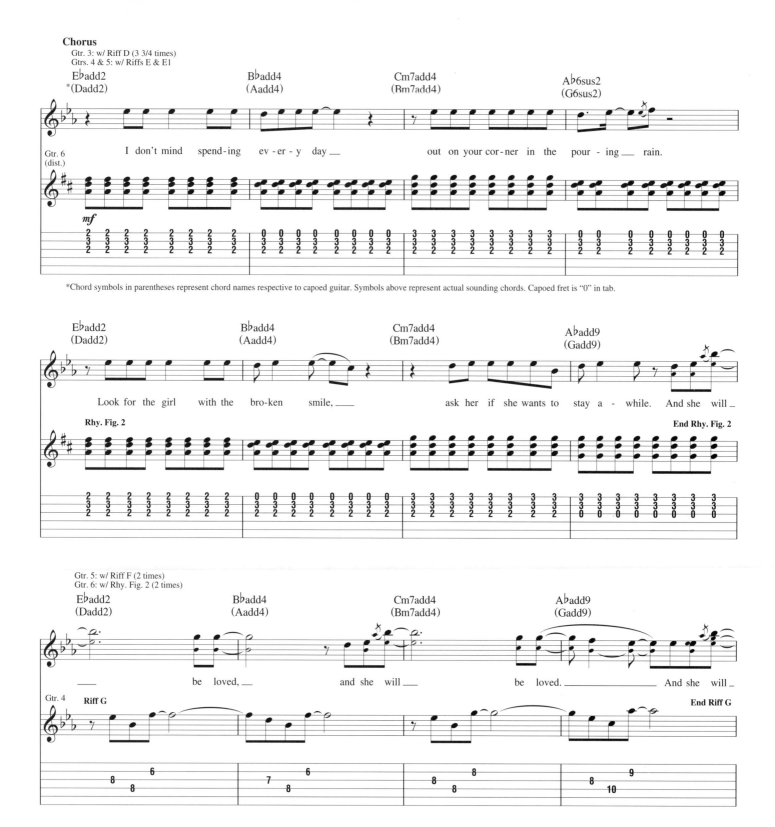

*Chord symbols in parentheses represent chord names respective to capoed guitar. Symbols above represent actual sounding chords. Capoed fret is "0" in tab.

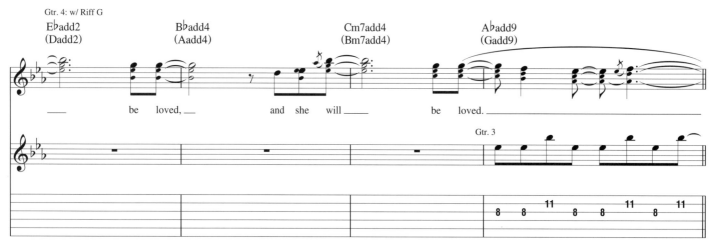

Bridge

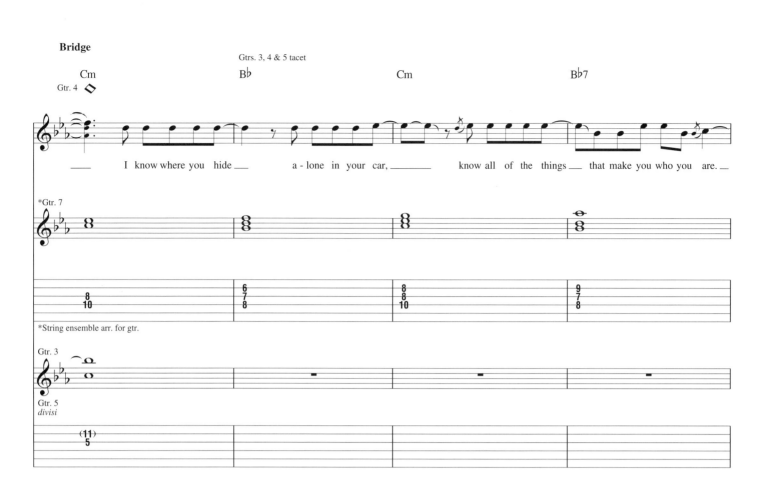

I know where you hide ___ a-lone in your car, _____ know all of the things ___ that make you who you are. ___

I know that good-bye _____ means noth-ing at all, ___ comes back and begs me catch her ev-'ry time ___ she ___

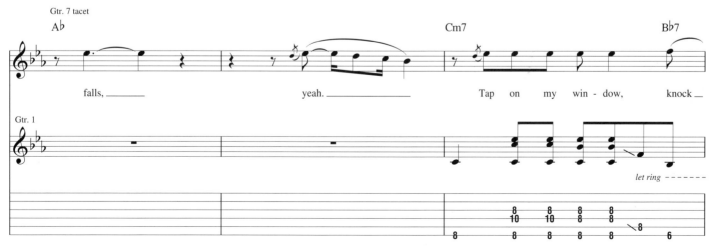

falls, _____ yeah. _____ Tap on my win-dow, knock ___

_____ on ___ my ___ door, ___ I ___ want ___ to ___ make ___ you ___ feel ___ beau - ti - ful. _____

let ring *let ring* *let ring*

Chorus
Gtr. 1 tacet
Gtr. 3: w/ Riff D (6 times)
Gtrs. 4 & 5: w/ Riffs E & E1

I ___ don't ___ mind ___ spend-ing ___ ev - er - y ___ day _____ out ___ on ___ your ___ cor - ner ___ in ___ the ___ pour-ing _____ rain, _____ oh. _____

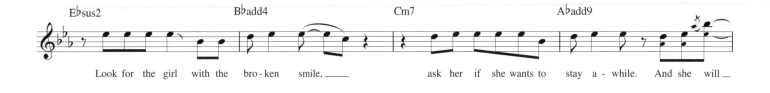

Look ___ for ___ the ___ girl ___ with ___ the ___ bro - ken ___ smile, _____ ask ___ her ___ if ___ she ___ wants ___ to ___ stay ___ a - while. ___ And ___ she ___ will _____

Gtr. 4: w/ Riff G (4 times)
Gtr. 5: w/ Riff F (4 times)

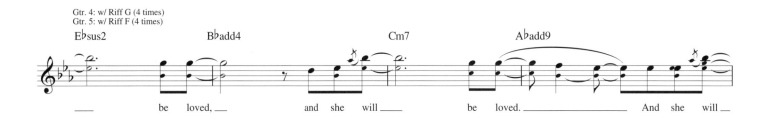

_____ be ___ loved, _____ and ___ she ___ will _____ be ___ loved. _____ And ___ she ___ will _____

_____ be ___ loved, _____ and ___ she ___ will _____ be ___ loved. _____

(Please ___ don't ___ try ___ so ___ hard ___ to ___ say ___ good -

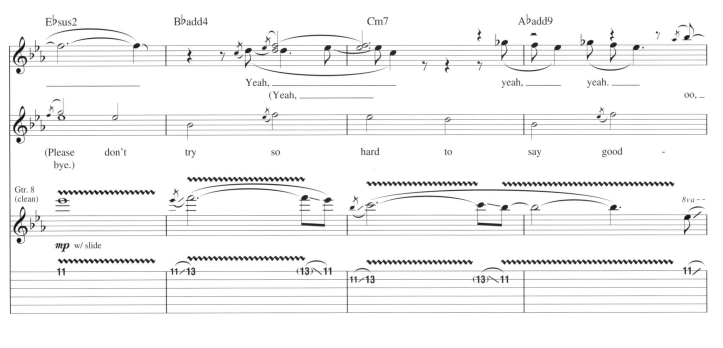

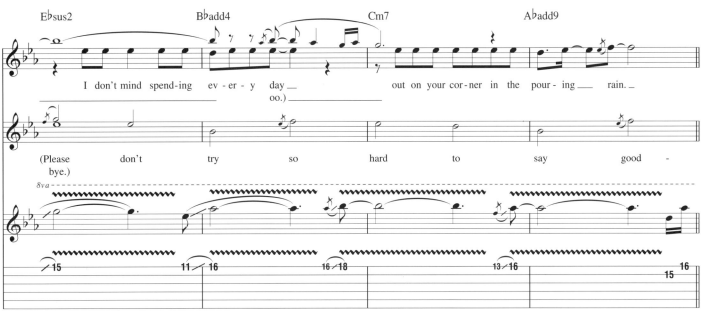

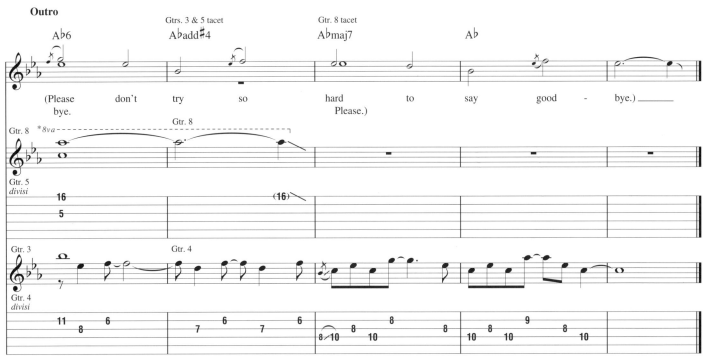

*Refers to Gtr. 8 only

Tangled

Words and Music by Adam Levine

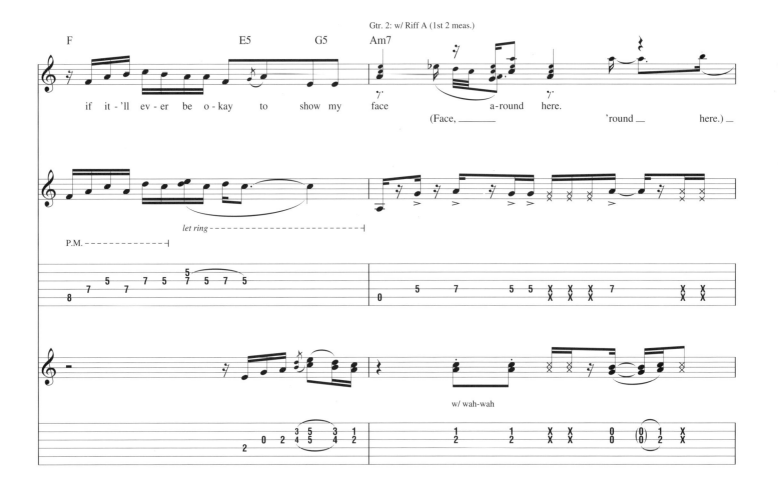

if it-'ll ev-er be o-kay to show my face a-round here. (Face, _____ 'round _____ here.) _____

Some-times I won-der if I dis-ap-pear, would you _____ ev-er turn _____ your head _____ and look, _____

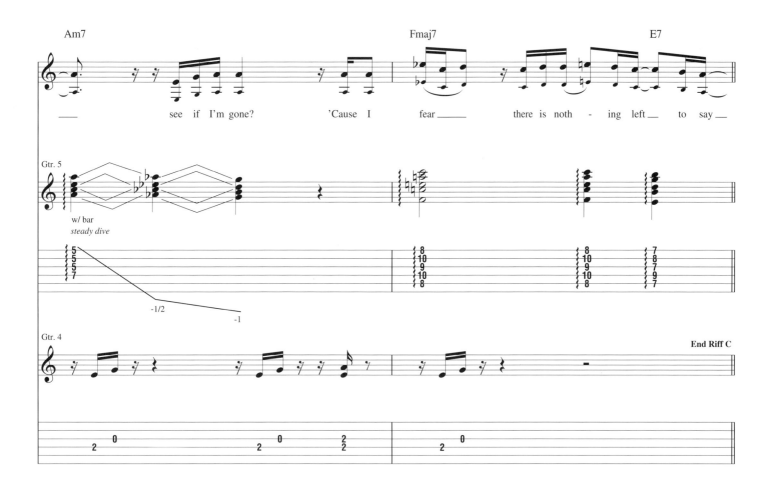

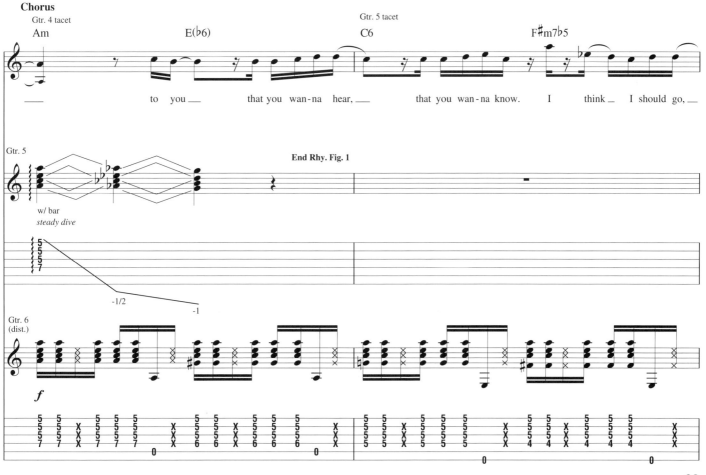

the things _ I have done _ are way _ too shame - ful, oh. _

Verse
Gtrs. 2 & 4: w/ Riffs A & A1
Gtr. 3: w/ Riff B (2 times)

2. You're just in - no- cent, a help - less vic - tim of a spi - der's web, and

Pre-Chorus

Gtrs. 1 & 7 tacet
Gtr. 4: w/ Riff C
Gtr. 5: w/ Rhy. Fig. 1

you _____ bet - ter turn _____ your head _____ and run, _____ and don't look back. 'Cause I

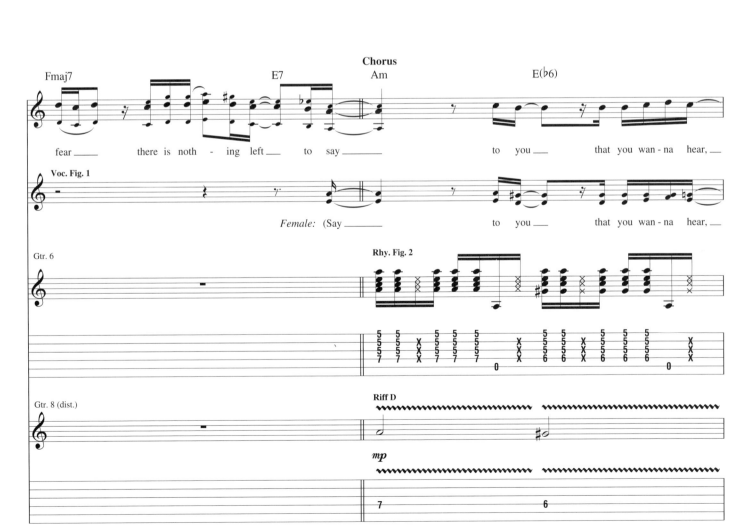

41

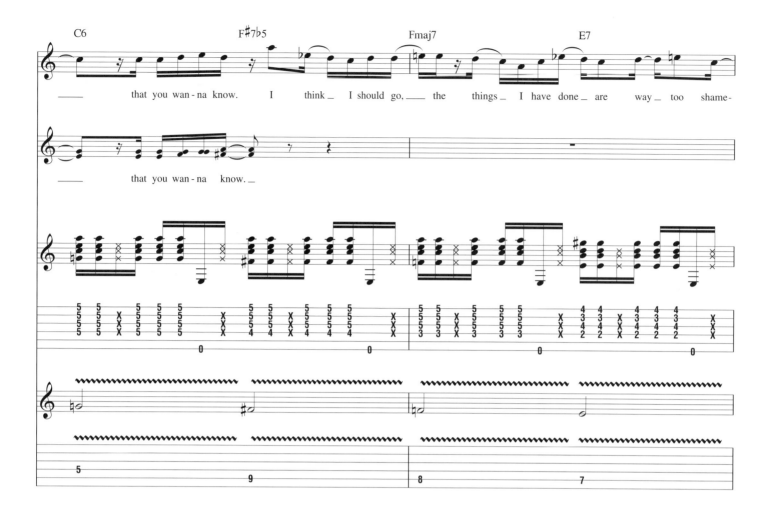

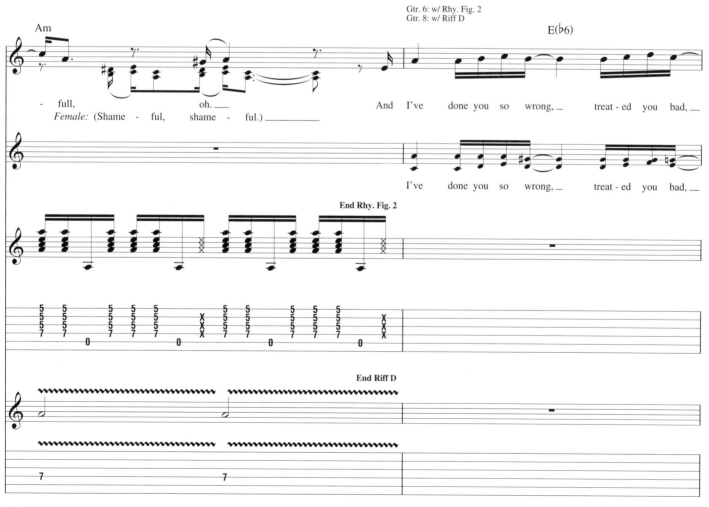

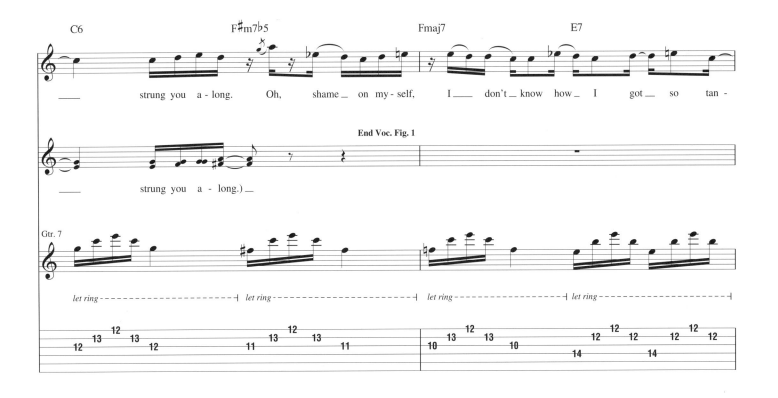

strung you a-long. Oh, shame__ on my-self, I__ don't__ know how__ I got__ so tan-

End Voc. Fig. 1

strung you a - long.)__

Bridge

- gled, oh.__ Mm, oh, oh, yeah,_____ yeah,__

Voc. Fig. 2

Male & Female: (Oo, oo, oo, oo,

Riff E

*Chord symbols reflect implied harmony.

**Sul ponticello - pick near the bridge.

*Chord symbols reflect overall harmony.

**Set pitch shifter to produce interval of a perfect 4th below with equal mix of processed (wet) and original (dry) signal.

Pre-Chorus

***Set for eighth-note regeneration.

Outro-Chorus

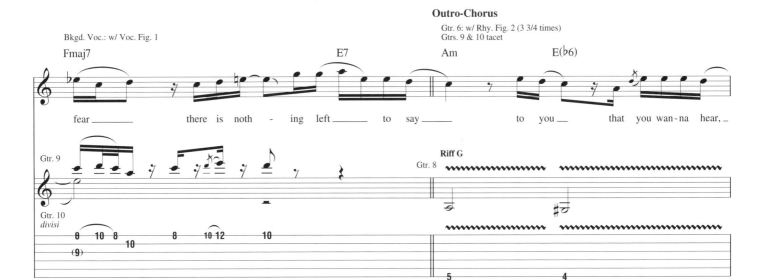

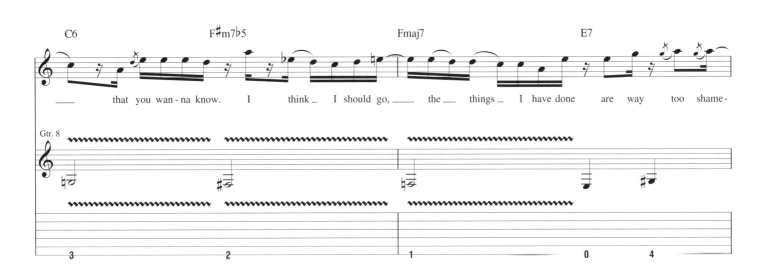

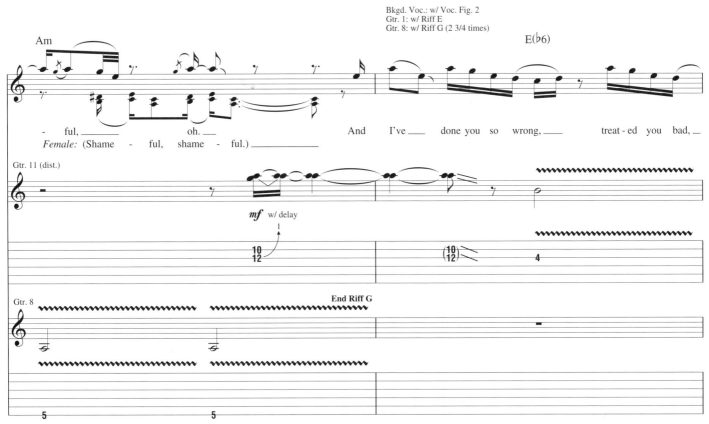

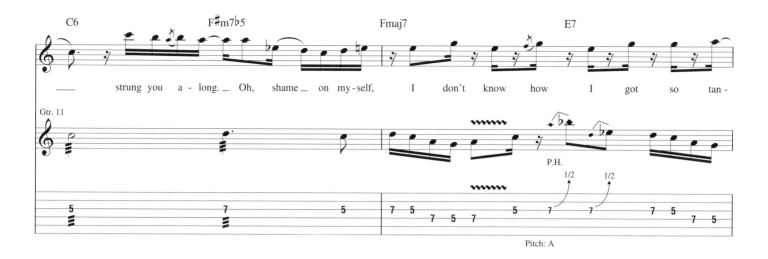

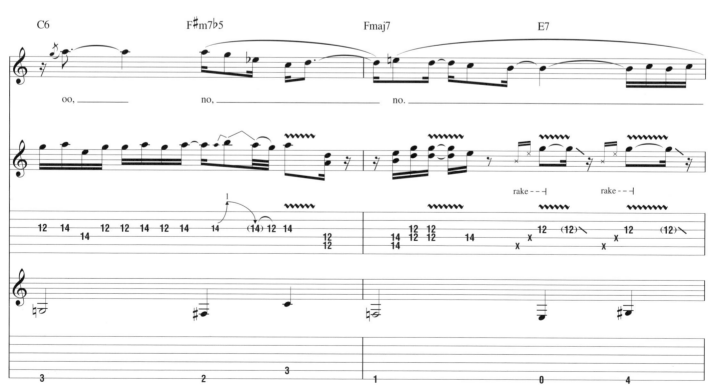

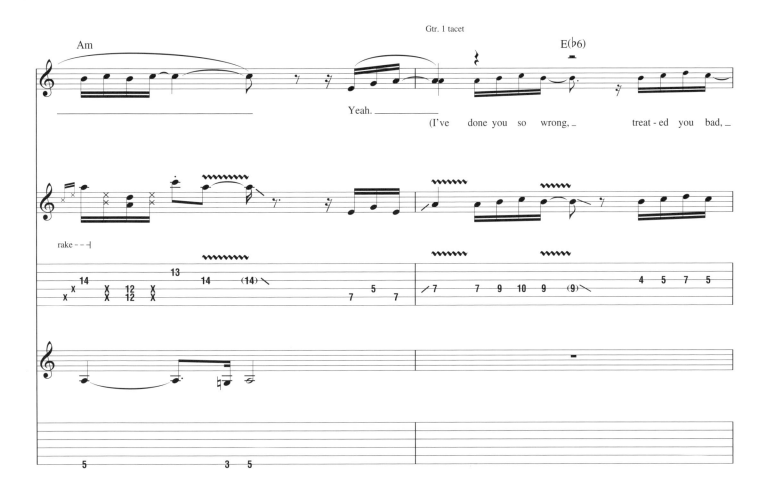

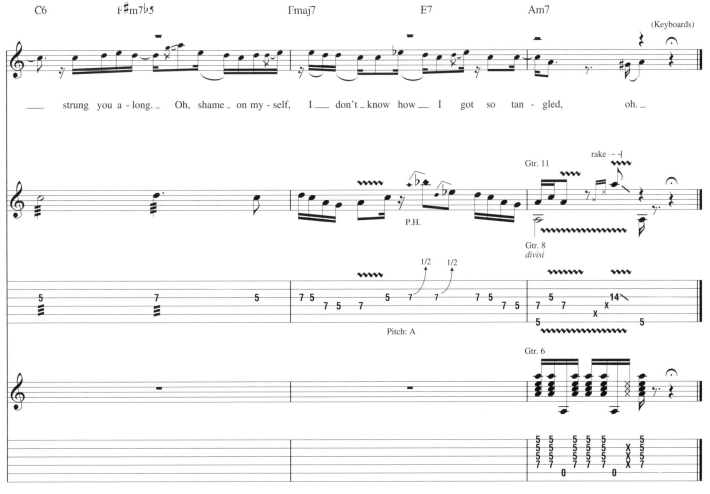

The Sun

Words and Music by Adam Levine

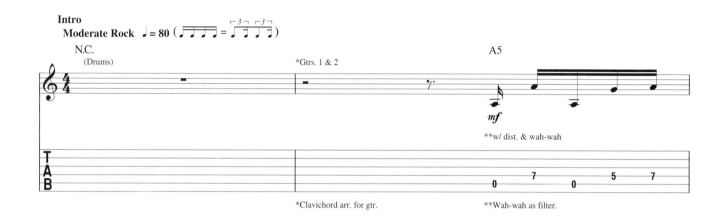

Intro
Moderate Rock ♩ = 80

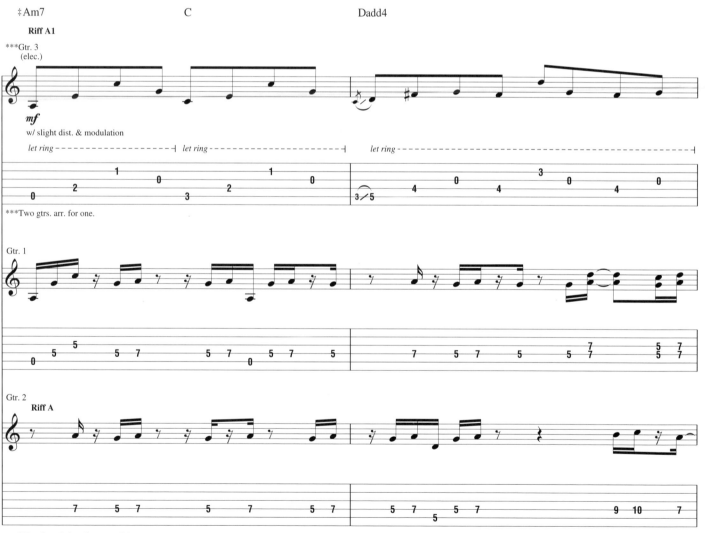

‡Chord symbols reflect overall harmony.

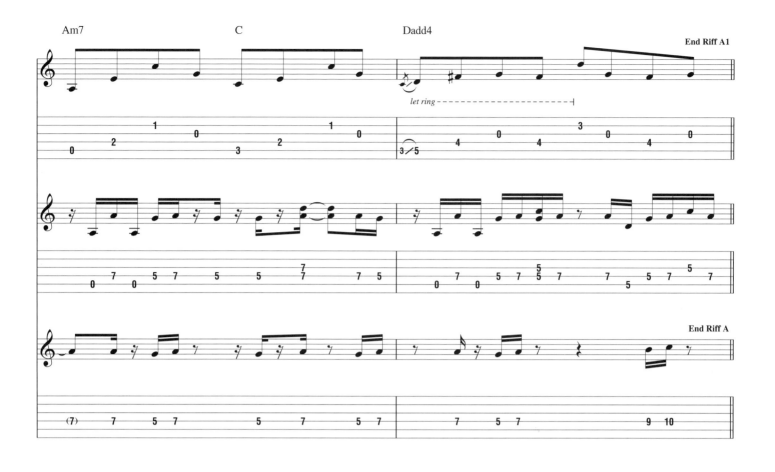

Verse
Gtrs. 2 & 3 tacet

1. Af - ter ___ school, ___ walk - ing ___ home, fresh dirt un - der my fin - ger - nails. ___ And

Gtr. 1 tacet

I can ___ smell _____ hot as - phalt, cars screech to a halt ___ to let me pass.

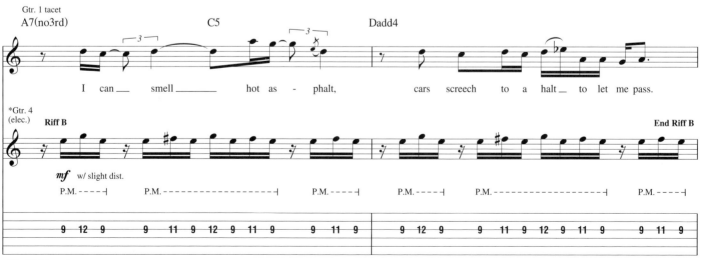

*Gtr. 4
(elec.)
Riff B

mf w/ slight dist.

*Doubled throughout

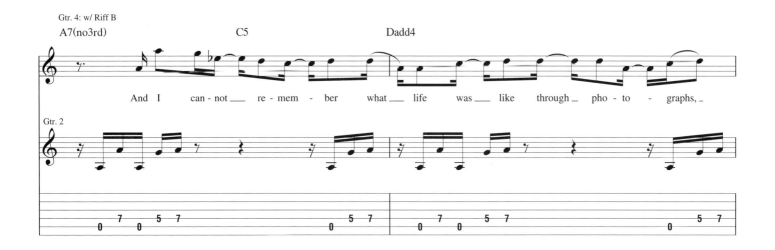

And I can-not ___ re-mem - ber what ___ life was ___ like through ___ pho-to - graphs, ___

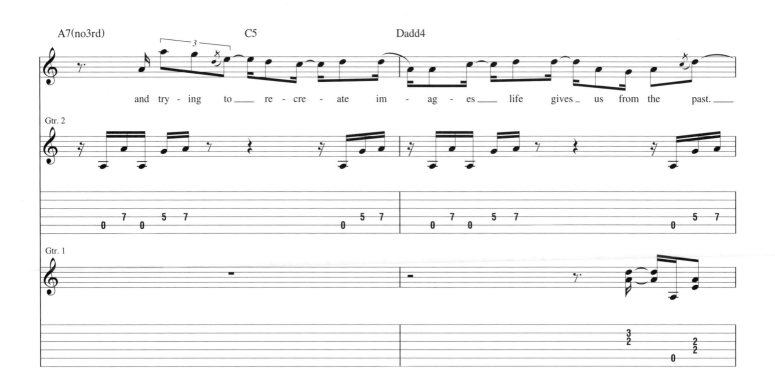

and try - ing to ___ re-cre-ate im - ag - es ___ life gives ___ us from the past. ___

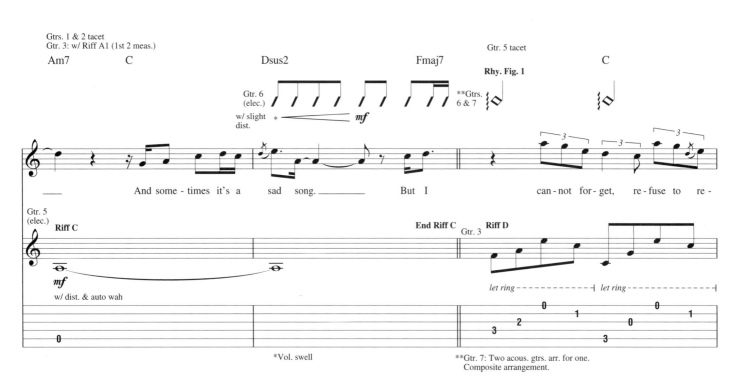

And some-times it's a sad song. ___ But I can-not for-get, re-fuse to re-

*Vol. swell

**Gtr. 7: Two acous. gtrs. arr. for one.
Composite arrangement.

50

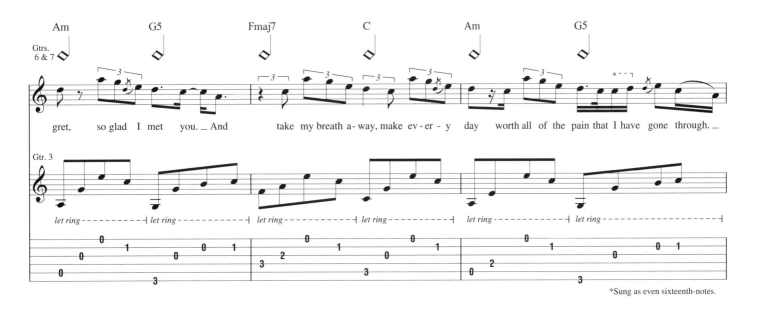

gret, so glad I met you. __ And take my breath a- way, make ev- er - y day worth all of the pain that I have gone through. __

*Sung as even sixteenth-notes.

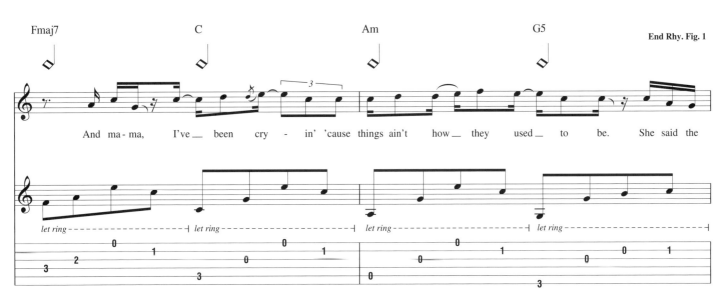

And ma - ma, I've __ been cry - in' 'cause things ain't how __ they used __ to be. She said the

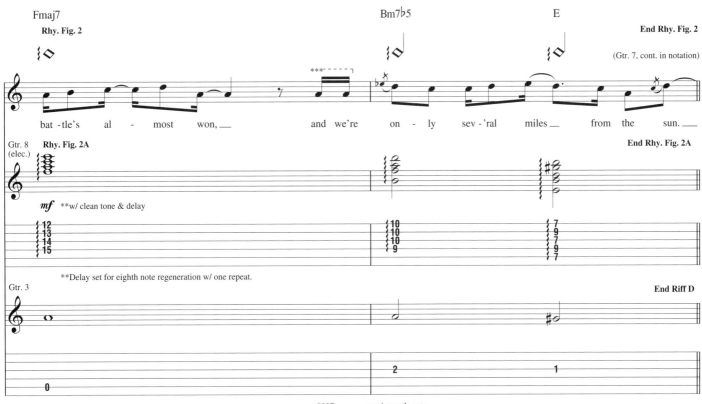

bat -tle's al - most won, __ and we're on - ly sev -'ral miles __ from the sun. __

**Delay set for eighth note regeneration w/ one repeat.

***Sung as even sixteenth-notes.

Interlude

Gtrs. 2 & 3: w/ Riffs A & A1
Gtrs. 6 & 8 tacet

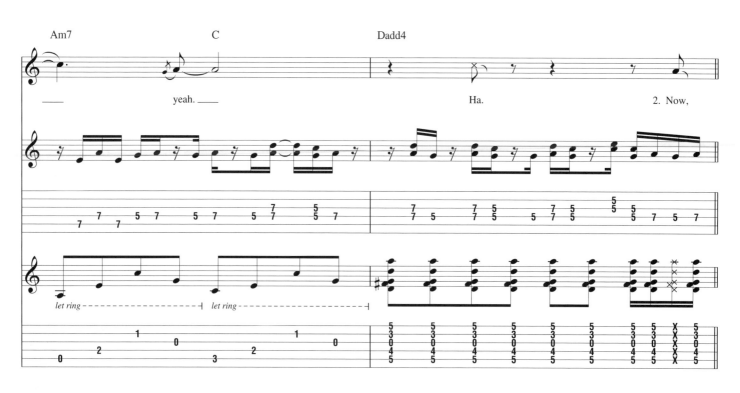

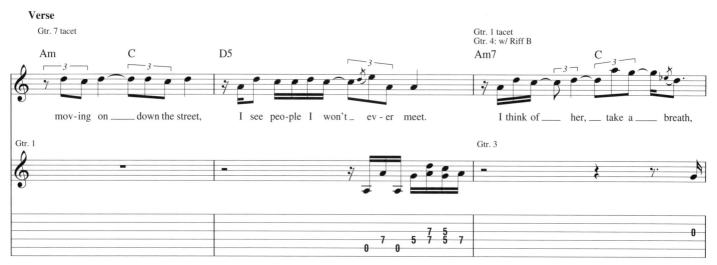

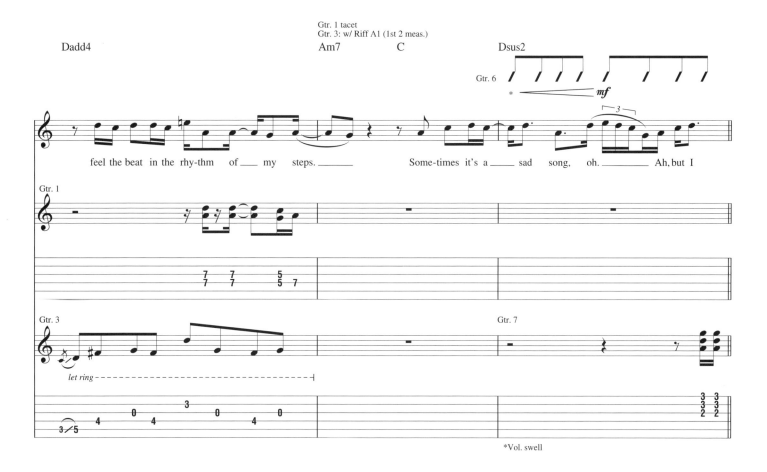

feel the beat in the rhy-thm of __ my steps. _____ Some-times it's a __ sad song, oh. _____ Ah, but I

*Vol. swell

Chorus

Gtr. 3: w/ Riff D
Gtr. 6: w/ Rhy. Fig. 1

can-not for - get, re-fuse to re - gret, so glad I met you. __ And take my breath a - way, make ev-er-y

day worth all of the pain that I have gone through. __ And ma - ma, I've __ been cry - in' 'cause

**Sung as even sixteenth notes.

things ain't how__ they used __ to be. She said the bat-tle's al - most won,_____ and we're

on - ly sev-'ral miles __ from the sun.__ The rhy-thm __ of her con-ver - sa - tion, the per - fec-tion of her cre - a - tion,

*Chord symbols reflect implied harmony.

**Gtr. 9: elec. w/ clean tone. Gtr. 10: Fender Rhodes piano arr. for gtr. Composite arrangement.

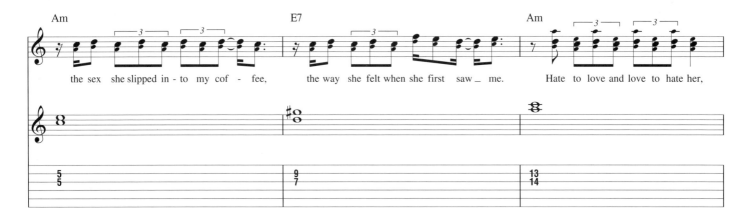

the sex she slipped in - to my cof - fee, the way she felt when she first saw __ me. Hate to love and love to hate her,

like a bro-ken rec-ord play- er, back and forth and here and gone __ and on _____ and on __ and on __ and on. _____
(Yeah.)

Chorus

Gtr. 3: w/ Riff D
Gtr. 6: w/ Rhy. Fig. 1
Gtr. 7: w/ Rhy. Fig. 3

___ I can-not for-get, re-fuse to re-gret, so glad I met you. And, _____ take my breath a-way, make ev-er-y
(My breath a-way, make ev-er-y

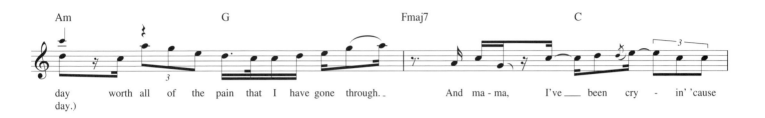

day worth all of the pain that I have gone through.___ And ma-ma, I've ___ been cry-in' 'cause
day.)

Gtrs. 6 & 7: w/ Rhy. Fig. 2 (2 times)
*Gtr. 8: w/ Rhy. Fig. 2A (2 times)

things ain't how ___ they used ___ to be.___ She said the bat-tle's al-most won, ___ and we're
*Delay off

Gtr. 3: w/ Riff D (last 2 meas.)

on-ly sev-'ral miles, _____ said the bat-tle's al-most won, _ and we're on-ly sev-'ral miles _ from the sun. _

Gtr. 11 (elec.)

mf w/ clean tone
let ring - - - - - - - -

Interlude

Gtr. 2: w/ Riff A
Gtr. 11 tacet

_____ Yeah, _____ oh. _____

Gtr. 3

let ring - - - - - -   let ring - - - - - -   let ring - - - -   let ring - - - - - -   let ring - - - - - -

**Chord symbols reflect overall harmony.

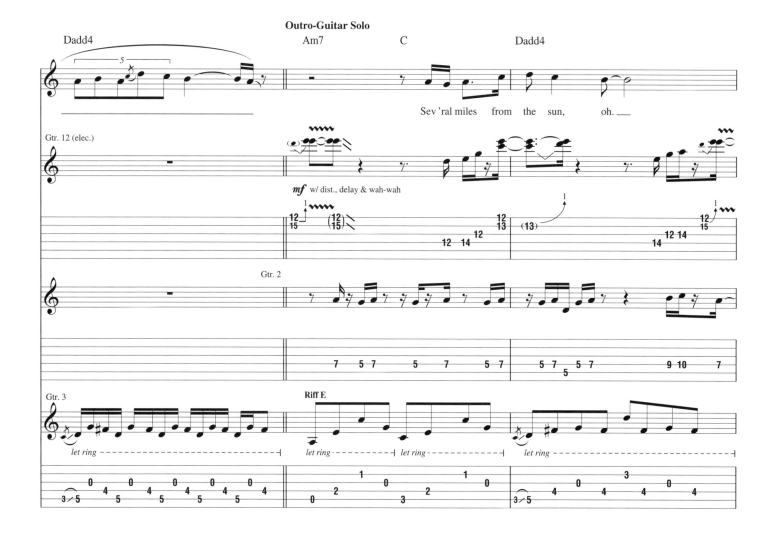

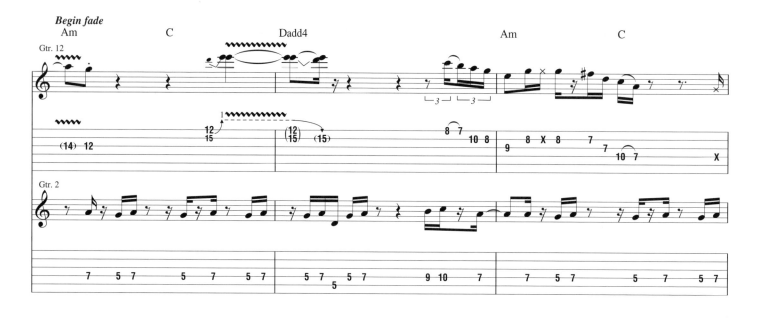

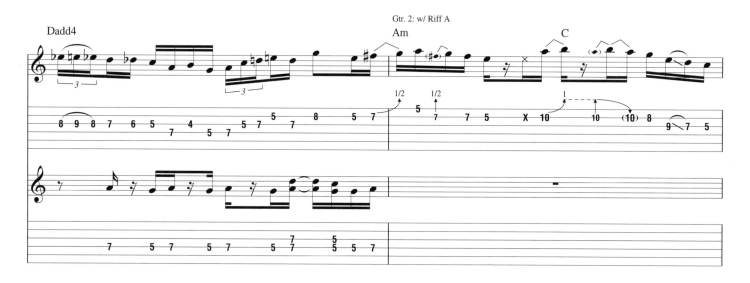

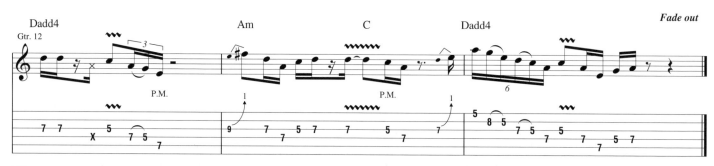

Must Get Out

Words and Music by Adam Levine and Jesse Carmichael

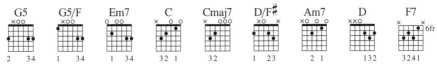

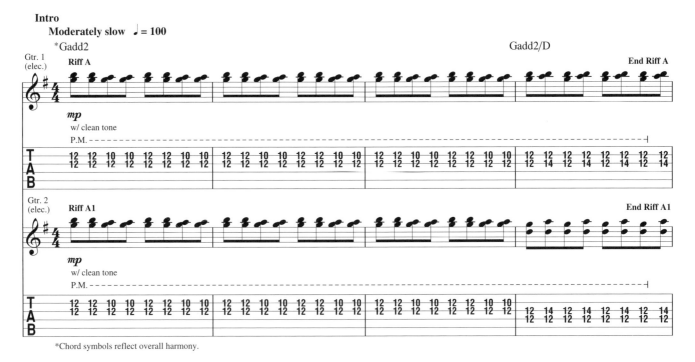

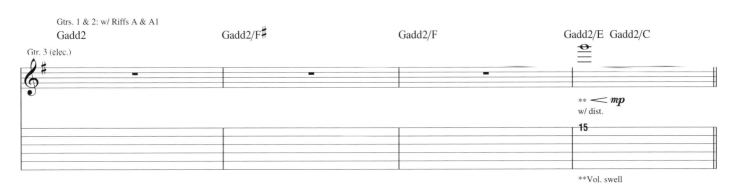

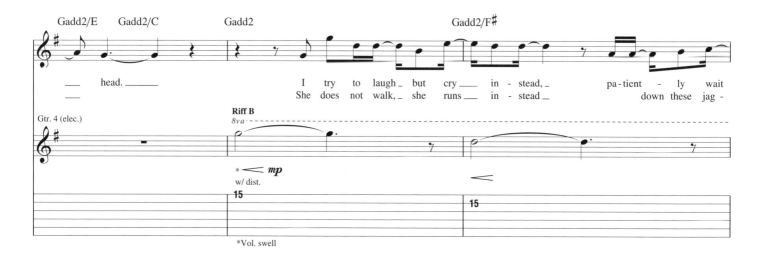

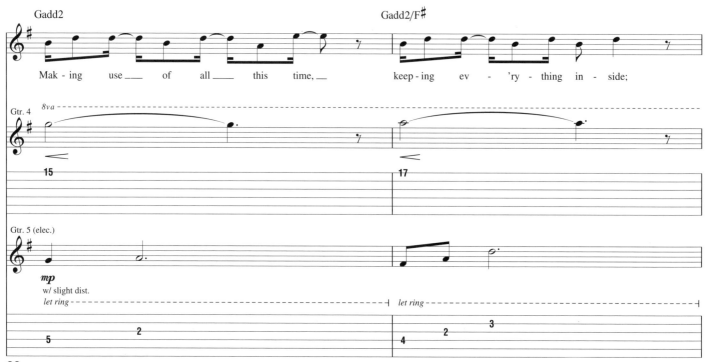

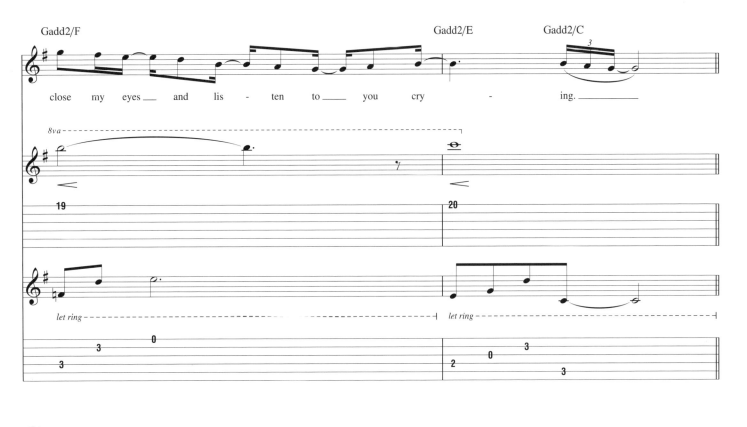

close my eyes ___ and lis - ten to ___ you cry - ing. ___

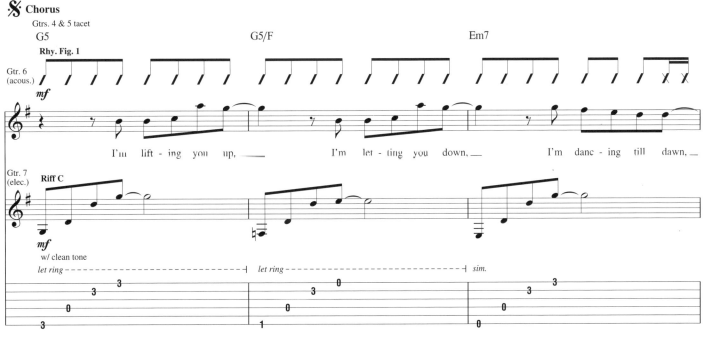

§ **Chorus**

Gtrs. 4 & 5 tacet

G5   G5/F   Em7

Rhy. Fig. 1

Gtr. 6
(acous.)

mf

I'm lift - ing you up, ___ I'm let - ting you down, ___ I'm danc - ing till dawn, ___

Gtr. 7
(elec.)

Riff C

mf
w/ clean tone

let ring - ┘ *let ring* - ┘ *sim.*

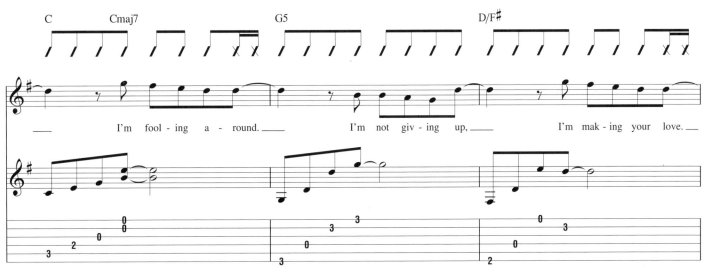

C Cmaj7   G5   D/F#

___ I'm fool - ing a - round. ___ I'm not giv - ing up, ___ I'm mak - ing your love.

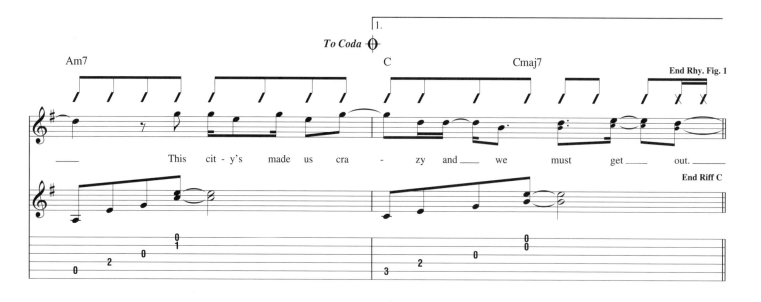

This cit-y's made us cra - zy and ___ we must get ___ out. ___

Interlude

Oh, ___ yeah, ___ now.

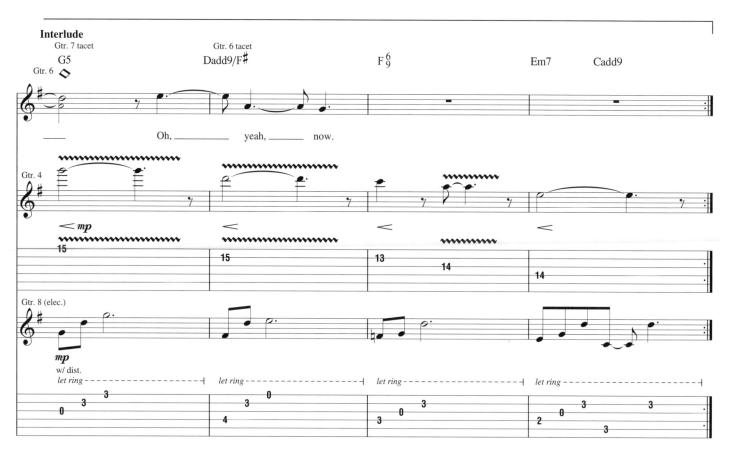

-zy and ___ we must get ___ out. There's on - ly so ___ much I ___ can do ___

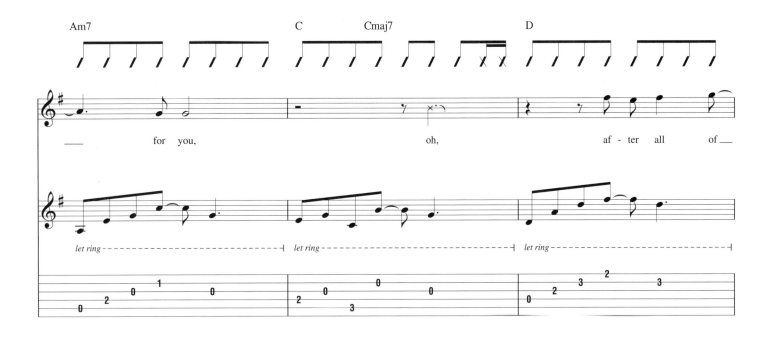

for you,　　　oh,　　　af - ter all of ___

let ring

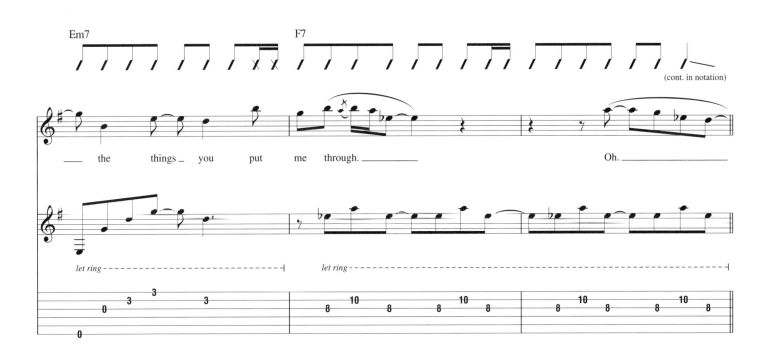

(cont. in notation)

___ the things ___ you put me through. _____　　　Oh. _____

let ring

let ring

Chorus

Gtrs. 6 & 7 tacet

Gtr. 9
(acous.)
mp

___ I'm lift-ing you up, ___　　I'm let-ting you down, ___　　I'm danc-ing till dawn, ___　　I'm fool-ing a - round. ___

Gtrs. 6 & 7

I'm not giv-ing up, ___ I'm mak-ing your love. ___ This cit-y's made us cra - zy and __ we must get ___ out. ___

⊕ Coda

- zy and __ we must get ___ out. ___ Whoa, ___ oh, ___ whoa, ___ oh, ___

(I'm lift-ing you up, ___ I'm let-ting you down, ___

___ whoa, ___ oh, ___ whoa, oh. ___ I'm danc-ing till dawn, ___ I'm fool-ing a - round. ___ I'm not giv-ing up, ___ I'm mak-ing your love. ___

Begin fade   Fade out

___ Yeah, ___ yeah, ___ yeah. ___

___ This cit-y's made us cra - zy and __ we must get ___ out.) ___

*w/ tremolo effect

64

Sunday Morning

Words and Music by Adam Levine and Jesse Carmichael

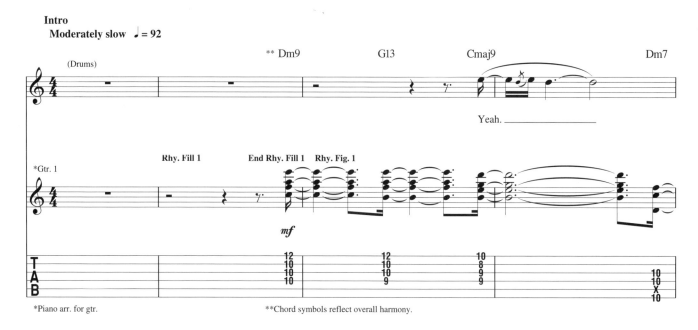

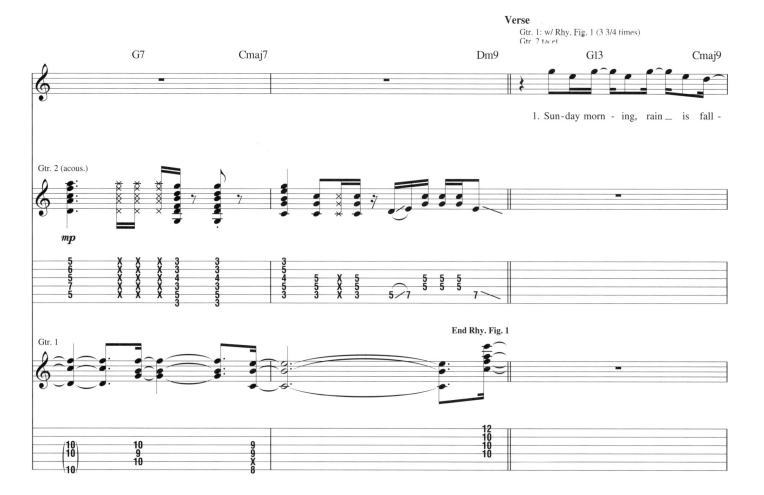

*Piano arr. for gtr.   **Chord symbols reflect overall harmony.

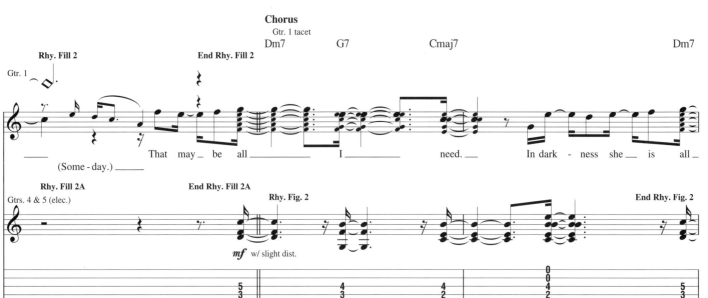

Gtrs. 4 & 5: w/ Rhy. Fig. 2 (2 times)

I see.
(You're all I see.)
Come and rest your bones with me.

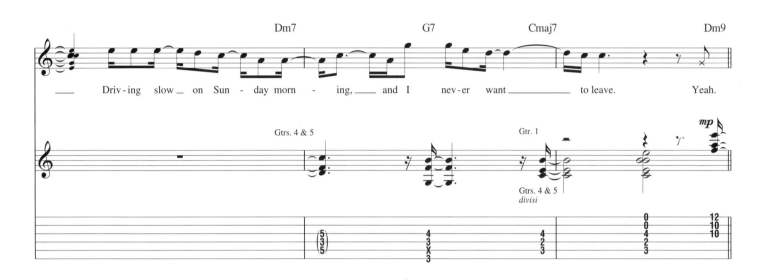

Driv-ing slow on Sun-day morn - ing, and I nev-er want to leave. Yeah.

Gtrs. 4 & 5

Gtr. 1

Gtrs. 4 & 5
divisi

Verse

Gtrs. 4 & 5 tacet
2nd time, Gtr. 1: w/ Rhy. Fig. 1
2nd time, Gtr. 6: w/ Riff B (4 times)

w/ Bkgd. Voc. ad lib.

1st time, Gtr. 3: w/ Riff A (3 times)
2nd time, Gtr. 3 tacet

2. Fin-gers trace your ev-'ry out - line, oh, yeah, yeah, paint a pic-ture with my hands.
__ just get __ so cra - zy, liv - ing life __ gets hard __ to do. __ Sun-day morn - ing, rain is fall-ing and __ I'm call -

Gtr. 1

Riff B
Gtr. 6 (elec.)

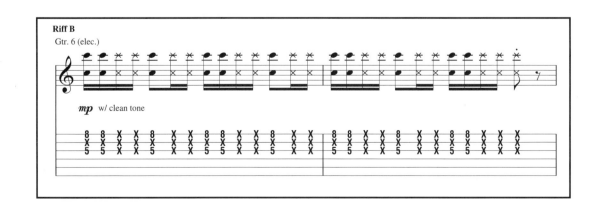

mp w/ clean tone

67

Gtr. 1: w/ Rhy. Fill 1

C   C#°7   Dm9

Oh, _____ yeah! _ 3. But things _

Gtrs. 4 & 5

Coda

Gtrs. 4 & 5: w/ Rhy. Fig. 2

Dm7   G7   Cmaj7

____ (Driv-ing slow _ on Sun-day morn-ing. _____)   Driv-ing slow... ___ Oh, yeah, _

Outro
w/ Lead Voc. ad lib.
Gtrs. 4 & 5: w/ Rhy. Fig. 2 (till fade)
Gtr. 6: w/ Riff B (till fade)

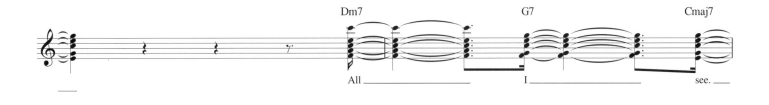

Dm7   G7   Cmaj7

____ yeah. _ Oh, yeah, _ yeah. _ Oh, yeah...
All _____ I _____ need. _

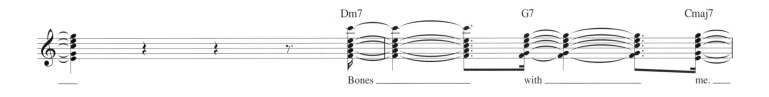

Dm7   G7   Cmaj7

All _____ I _____ see. _

Dm7   G7   Cmaj7

____ Bones _____ with _____ me. _

Play 3 times and fade

G7   Dm7   G7   Cmaj7   Dm7

____ Driv-ing home _ on Sun-day morn-ing. _ All _

Secret

Words and Music by Adam Levine and Jesse Carmichael

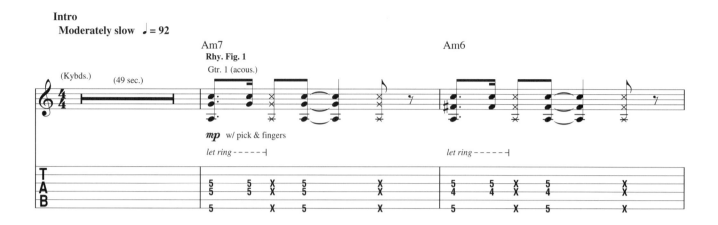

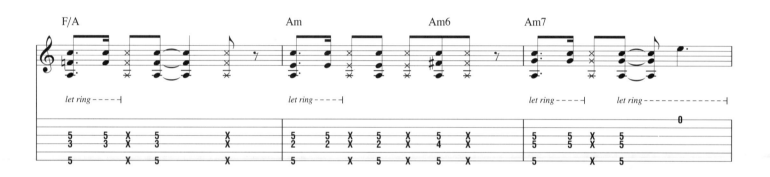

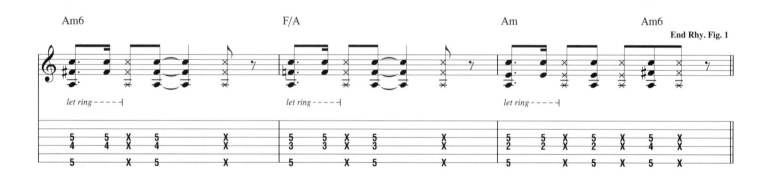

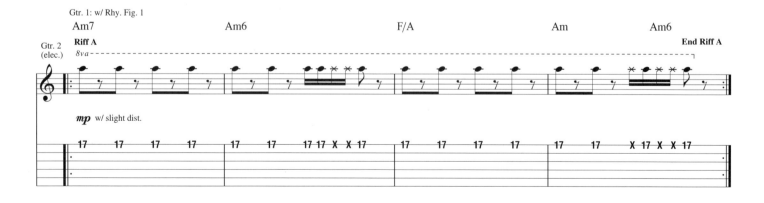

Verse
Gtr. 2 tacet

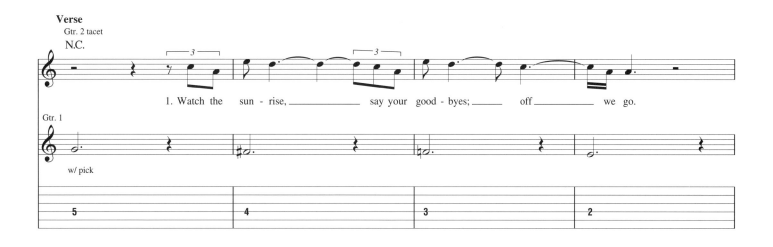

1. Watch the sun - rise, _____ say your good - byes; _____ off _____ we go.

w/ pick

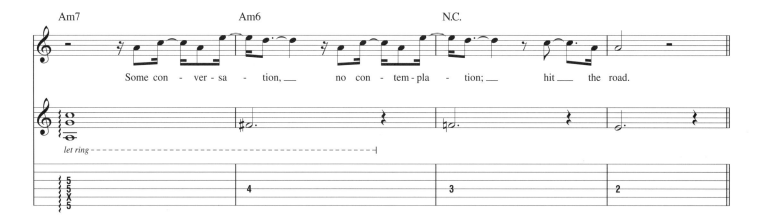

Some con - ver - sa - tion, ___ no con - tem - pla - tion; ___ hit ___ the road.

let ring

Pre-Chorus
Gtr. 1: w/ Rhy. Fig. 1
Gtr. 2: w/ Riff A (2 times)

Car o - ver - heats, jump out of my seat on the side of the high - way, ba - by.

Our road is long, your hold is strong. Please don't ev - er let go, oh, ___ no.

Chorus

I know I _____ don't know you, ___ but I want you ___ so ___ bad. _____

Rhy. Fig. 2
Gtr. 1

End Rhy. Fig. 2

w/ pick & fingers
*T   T

let ring   let ring   let ring   let ring

*T = Thumb on 6th string

71

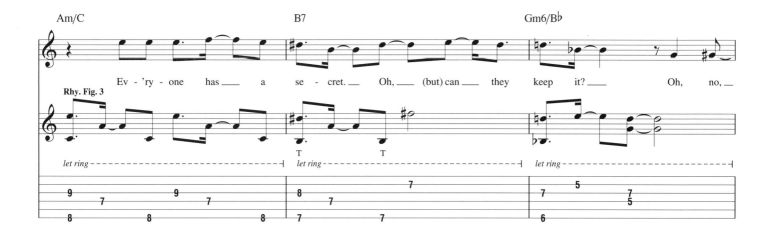

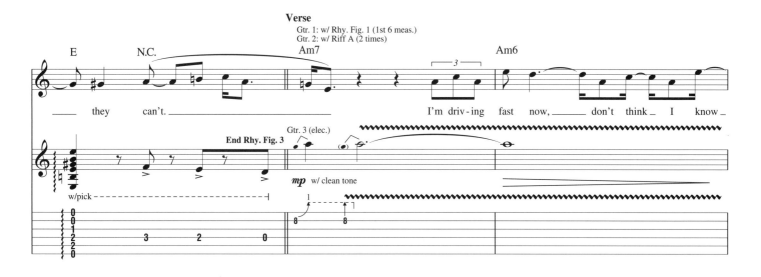

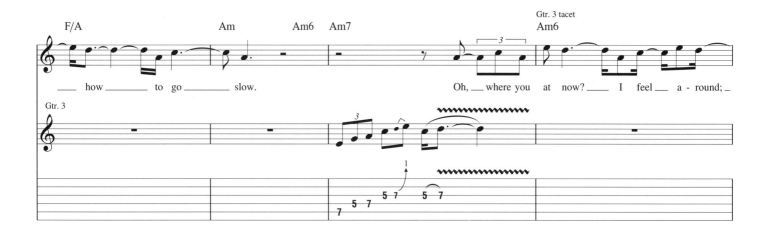

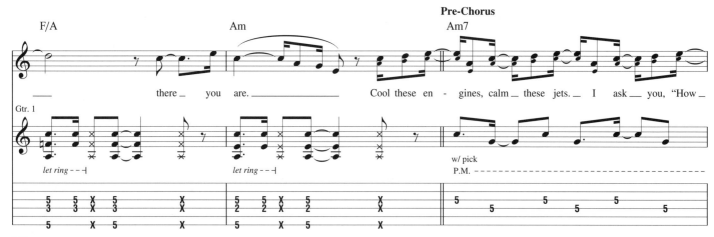

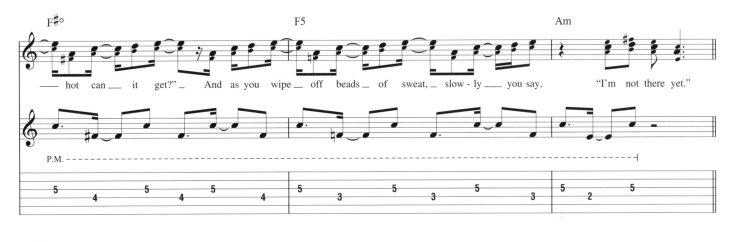

hot can ___ it get?"___ And as you wipe ___ off beads ___ of sweat, slow - ly ___ you say, "I'm not there yet."

P.M. -

Chorus
Gtr. 1: w/ Rhy. Fig. 2

*Voc. Fig. 1

I know I ___ don't know you, ___ but I want you ___ so ___ bad. ___
(Ah,   ah,   ah.

*Refers to downstemmed notes only.

Gtr. 1: w/ Rhy. Fig. 3

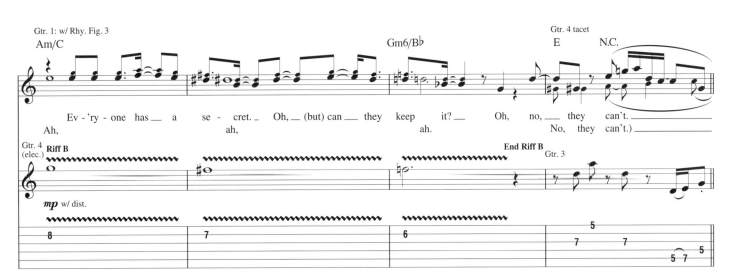

Ev - 'ry - one has ___ a se - cret. ___ Oh, ___ (but) can ___ they keep it? ___ Oh, no, ___ they can't. ___
Ah,   ah,   ah.   No, they can't.) ___

Gtr. 4 (elec.) **Riff B**   **End Riff B**   Gtr. 3

mp w/ dist.

Interlude

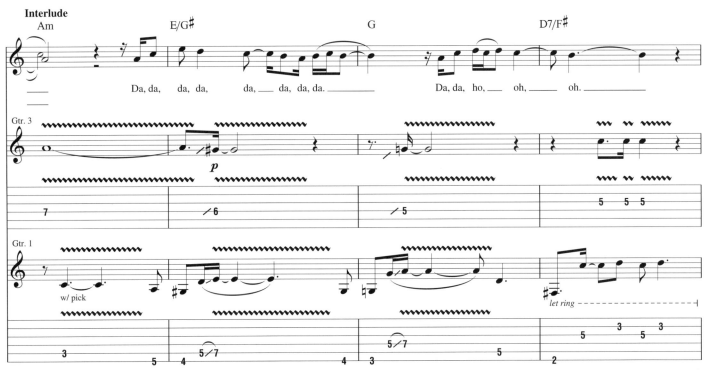

Da, da, da, da, da, ___ da, da, da. ___ Da, da, ho, ___ oh, ___ oh.

Gtr. 3

p

Gtr. 1

w/ pick   *let ring* - - - - - - - - - - - - - - - -

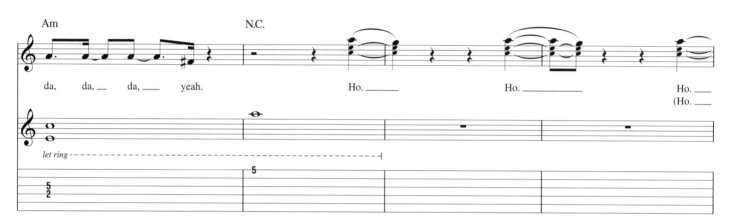

Through With You

Words and Music by Adam Levine and Jesse Carmichael

Tune down 1/2 step:
(low to high) Eb-Ab-Db-Gb-Bb-Eb

Intro
Slowly ♩ = 74

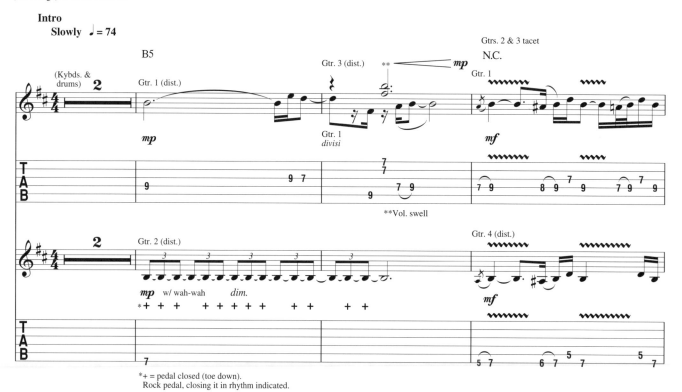

*+ = pedal closed (toe down).
  Rock pedal, closing it in rhythm indicated.

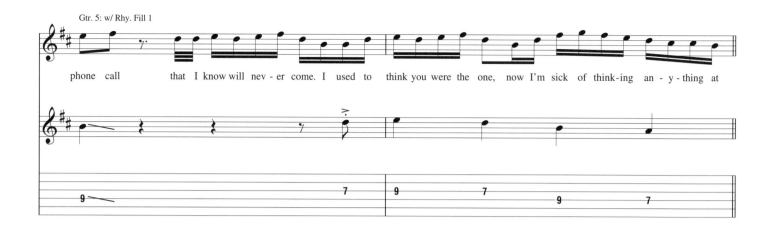

phone call　　　　that I know will nev - er come. I used to　think you were the one,　now I'm sick of think-ing　an - y - thing at

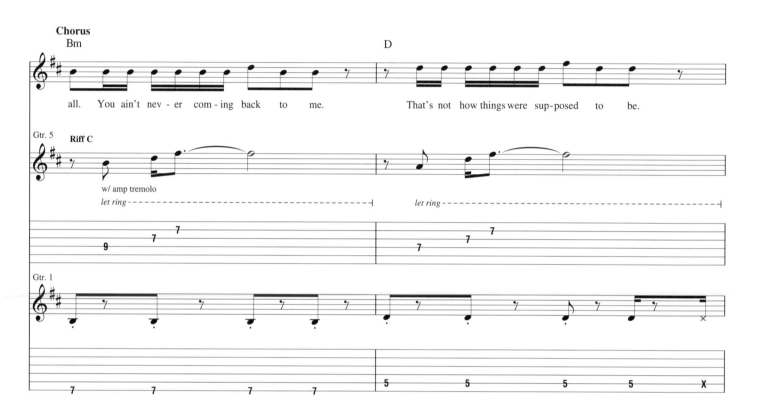

Chorus

Bm　　　　　　　　　　　　　　　　　　　　D

all.　You ain't nev - er com - ing back　to　me.　　　That's not　how things were sup - posed　to　be.

Gtr. 5 **Riff C**

w/ amp tremolo

let ring - ┘　　　　*let ring* - ┘

Gtr. 1

Em7　　　　　　　　　　　　　　　　　　　F#

You take my hand　just to give　it　back. _　　No oth - er lov - er has　ev - er done　that. 3. Do you re -

End Riff C

let ring - ┘　　　　*let ring* - ┘

(cont. in slashes)

78

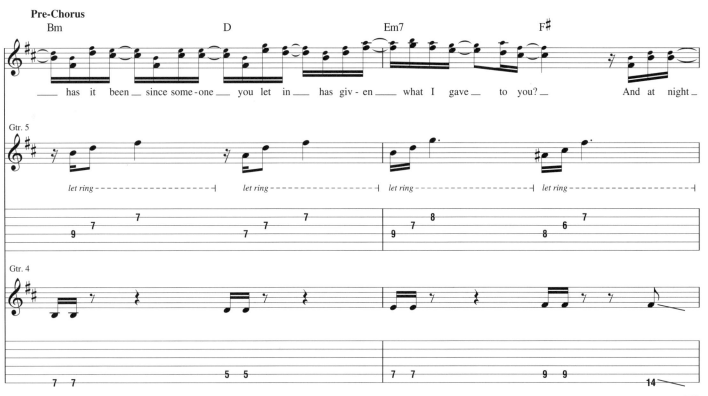

when you sleep, do you dream I would be there just for a min-ute or two? Do you?

let ring -   *let ring - - - - - - - - - - - - - - -*

𝄋 Chorus

Gtrs. 1 & 5: w/ Riff C (1 3/4 times)

* Voc. Fig. 1

You ain't nev-er com-in' back to me.
Oh,   oh,   oh.

That's not how things were sup-posed to be.
Oh,   oh,   oh.

Gtrs. 2 & 4

*Refers to upstemmed notes only.

End Voc. Fig. 1

You take my hand just to give it back. ___
Oh,   oh,   oh.

No oth-er lov-er has ev-er done that. _____
Oh,   oh,   oh.

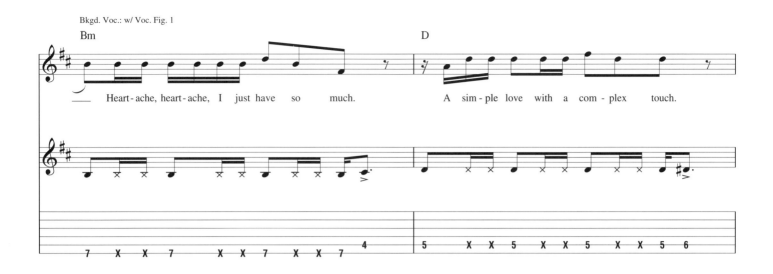

Bkgd. Voc.: w/ Voc. Fig. 1

Heart - ache, heart - ache, I just have so much. A sim - ple love with a com - plex touch.

To Coda ✛

Em7   N.C.   Bm   N.C.

Gtr. 5   (cont. in notation)

And there is noth-ing you can say or do. I called to let you know I'm through with you. Oh, ho.

Interlude

N.C.

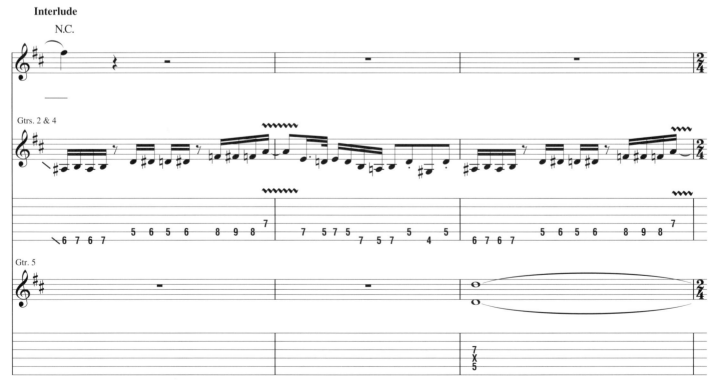

Gtrs. 2 & 4

Gtr. 5

F#

Coda

N.C.

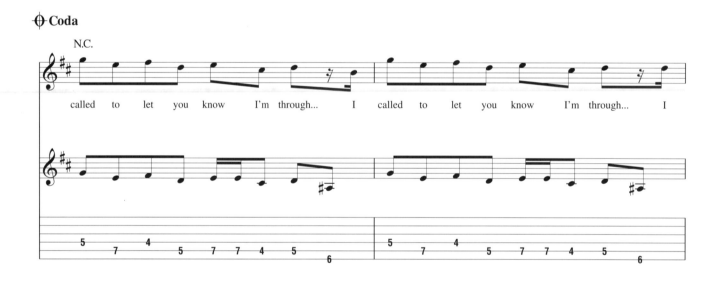

called to let you know I'm through... I called to let you know I'm through... I

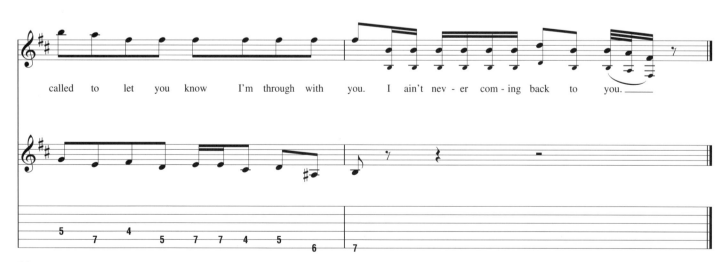

called to let you know I'm through with you. I ain't nev-er com-ing back to you. ___

Not Coming Home

Words and Music by Adam Levine, Jesse Carmichael and Ryan Dusick

What makes you think I'll let you in a - gain? ___
to say these things that I don't want to say, but have to say them an - y - way. ___

Think a - gain, ___ my friend. Go on, mis - use ___ me and a - buse me. ___
Oh. ___ I would do an - y - thing ___ to end your suf - fer - ing. ___

I'll come out strong - er in ___ the
But you would rath - er walk a -

To Coda ⊕

Chorus

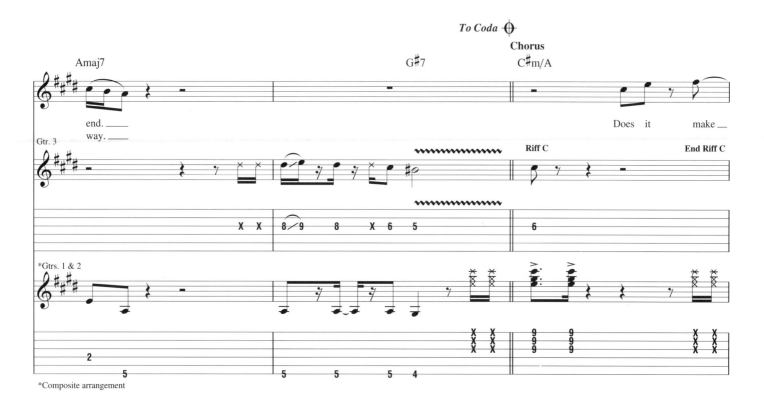

end. ___ Does it make ___
way. ___

you sad to find your - self a - lone? ___

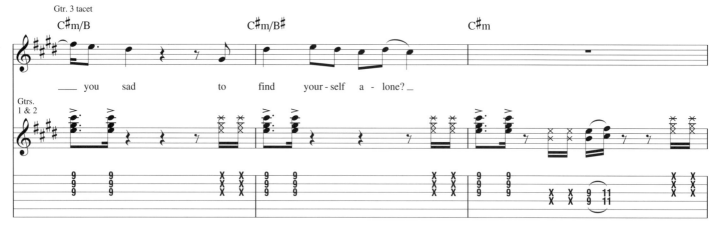

*Composite arrangement

84

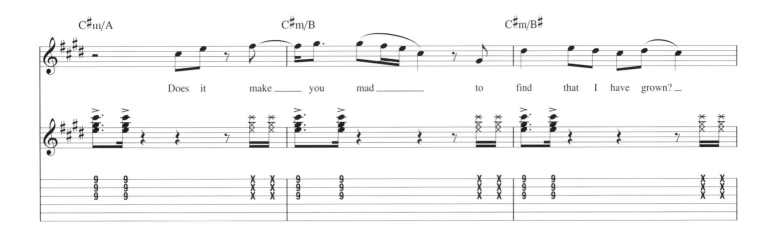

Does it make you mad to find that I have grown?

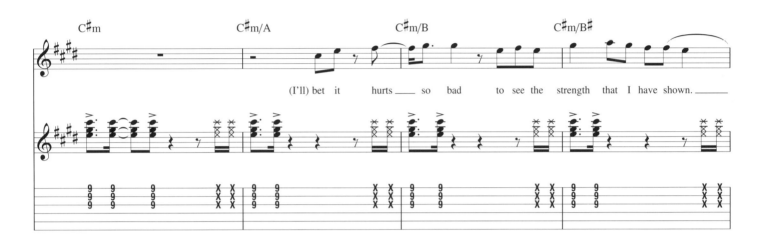

(I'll) bet it hurts so bad to see the strength that I have shown.

When you an-swer the door, pick up the phone, you won't

Interlude

D.S. al Coda

Gtrs. 1, 2 & 3: w/ Riffs A & A1

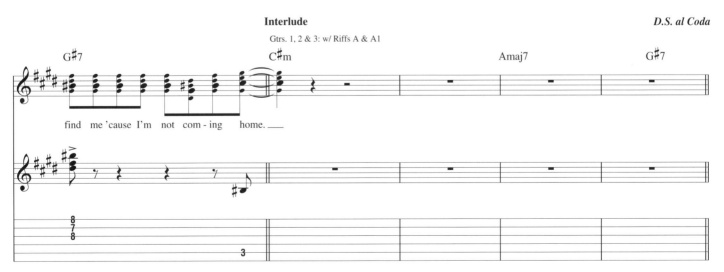

find me 'cause I'm not com-ing home.

⊕ Coda

Chorus

Gtr. 3: w/ Riff C

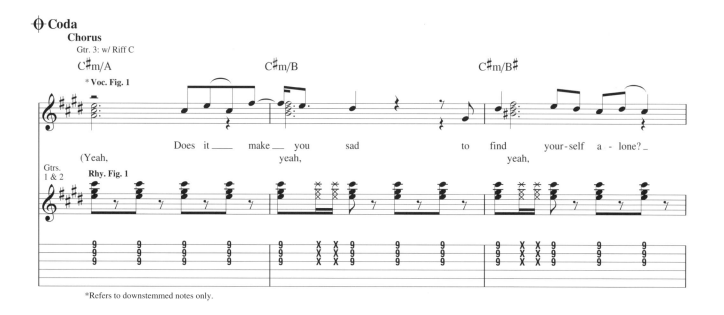

Does it ___ make ___ you sad to find your-self a - lone?___

(Yeah, yeah, yeah,

Gtrs. 1 & 2

*Refers to downstemmed notes only.

Bkgd. Voc.: w/ Voc. Fig. 1 (2 times)

And does it ___ make ___ you mad ___ to find that I have grown?___

yeah.)

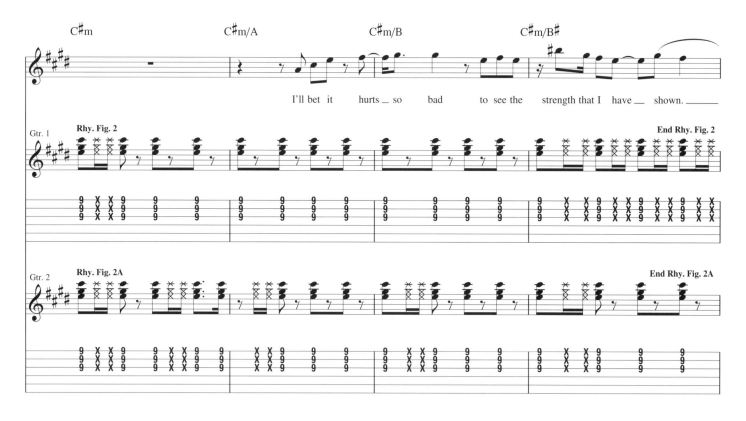

I'll bet it hurts ___ so bad to see the strength that I have ___ shown. ___

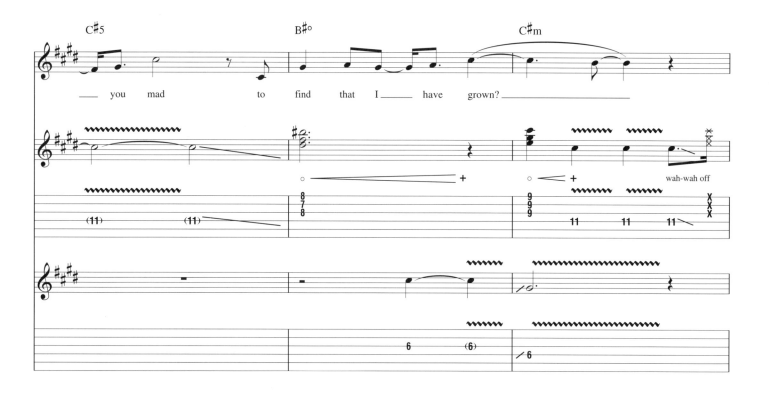

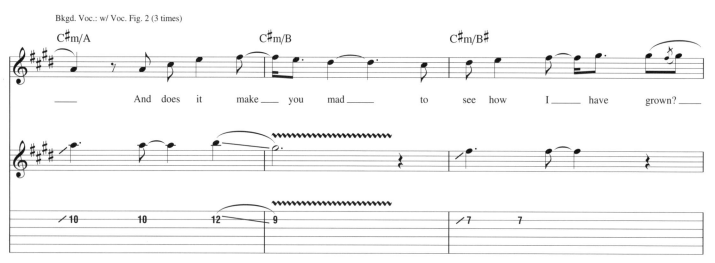

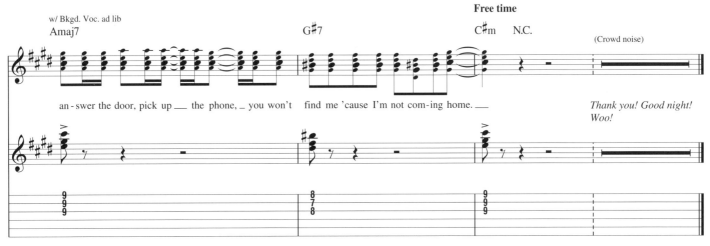

Sweetest Goodbye

Words and Music by Adam Levine

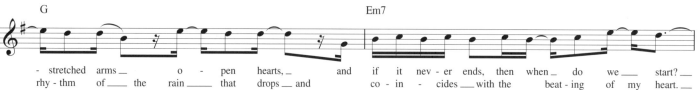

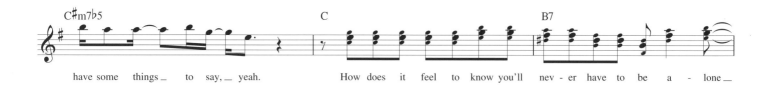

have some things _ to say, _ yeah.   How does it feel to know you'll nev-er have to be a - lone _

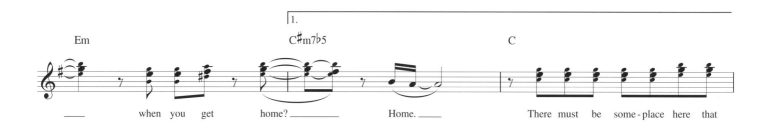

1.

_ when you get home? _____ Home. _____   There must be some-place here that

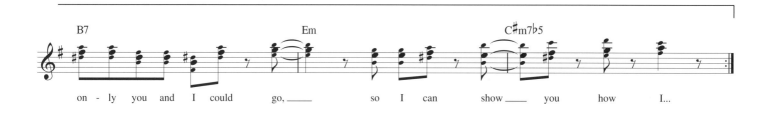

on - ly you and I could go, _____ so I can show _____ you how I...

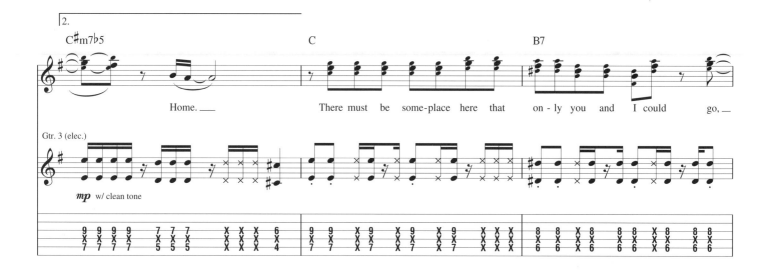

2.

Home. _____   There must be some-place here that on - ly you and I could go, _

Gtr. 3 (elec.)

mp w/ clean tone

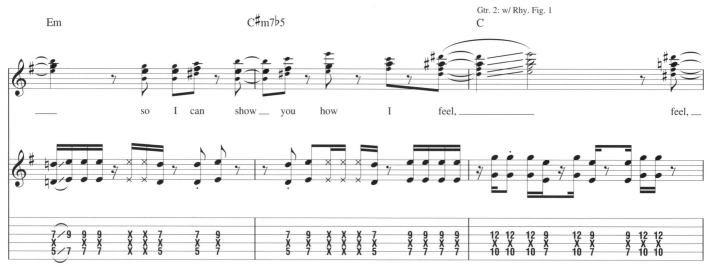

_ so I can show _ you how I feel, _____ feel, _

Gtr. 2: w/ Rhy. Fig. 1

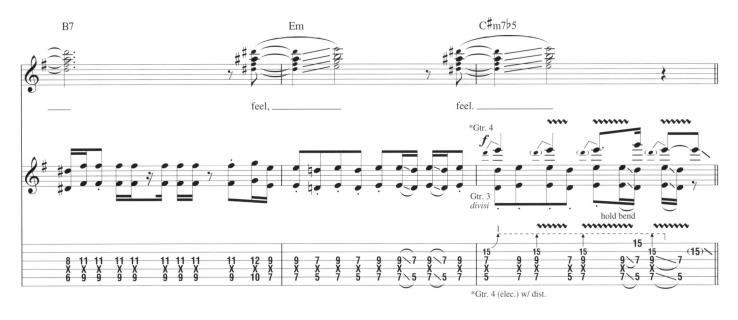

Outro - Guitar Solo
w/ Lead Voc. ad lib (till fade)
Gtr. 2: w/ Rhy. Fig. 1 (till fade)
Gtr. 3 tacet

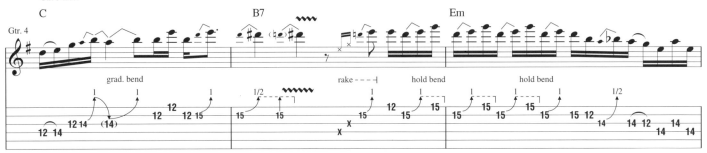

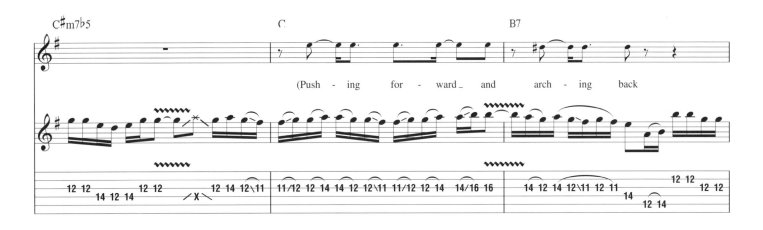

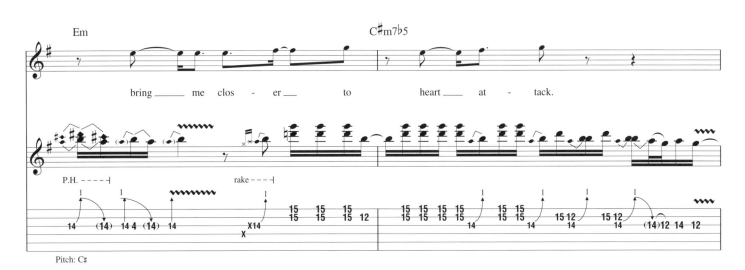

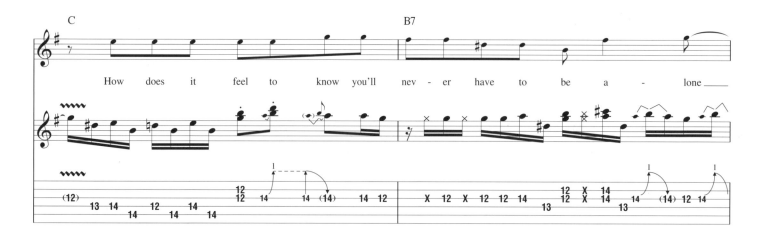

How does it feel to know you'll nev - er have to be a - lone ____

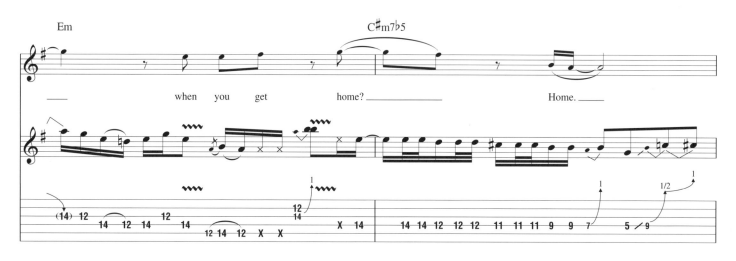

____ when you get home? ____ Home. ____

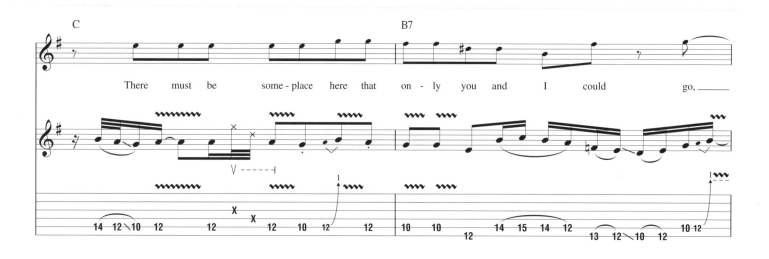

There must be some - place here that on - ly you and I could go, ____

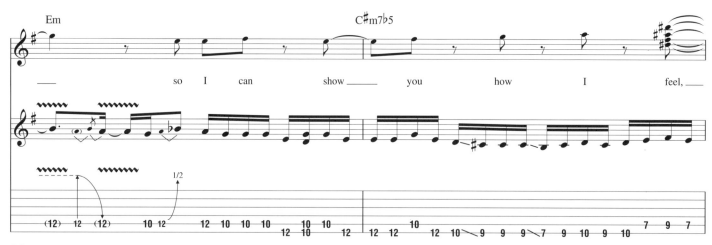

so I can show ____ you how I feel, ____

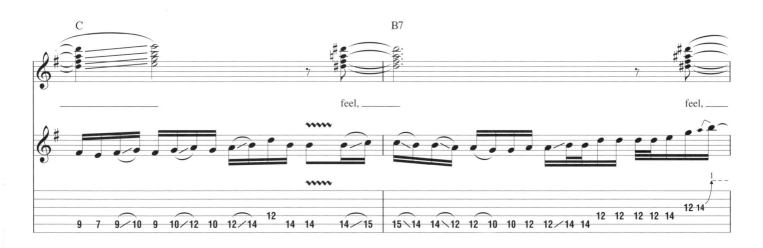

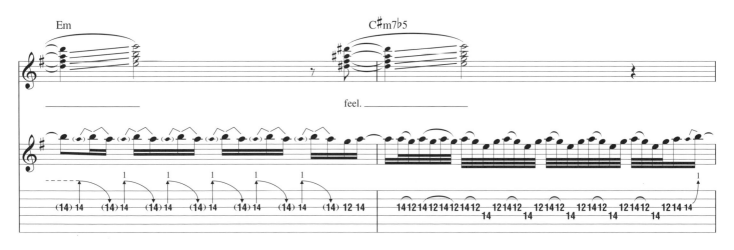

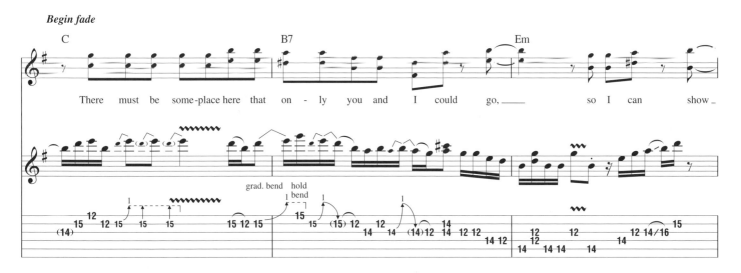

*Both bends executed w/ R.H. ring finger.

Guitar Notation Legend

Guitar Music can be notated three different ways: on a *musical staff*, in *tablature*, and in *rhythm slashes*.

RHYTHM SLASHES are written above the staff. Strum chords in the rhythm indicated. Use the chord diagrams found at the top of the first page of the transcription for the appropriate chord voicings. Round noteheads indicate single notes.

THE MUSICAL STAFF shows pitches and rhythms and is divided by bar lines into measures. Pitches are named after the first seven letters of the alphabet.

TABLATURE graphically represents the guitar fingerboard. Each horizontal line represents a string, and each number represents a fret.

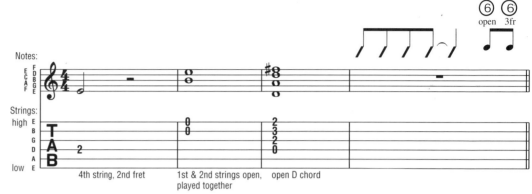

HALF-STEP BEND: Strike the note and bend up 1/2 step.

WHOLE-STEP BEND: Strike the note and bend up one step.

GRACE NOTE BEND: Strike the note and immediately bend up as indicated.

SLIGHT (MICROTONE) BEND: Strike the note and bend up 1/4 step.

BEND AND RELEASE: Strike the note and bend up as indicated, then release back to the original note. Only the first note is struck.

PRE-BEND: Bend the note as indicated, then strike it.

VIBRATO: The string is vibrated by rapidly bending and releasing the note with the fretting hand.

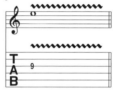

WIDE VIBRATO: The pitch is varied to a greater degree by vibrating with the fretting hand.

HAMMER-ON: Strike the first (lower) note with one finger, then sound the higher note (on the same string) with another finger by fretting it without picking.

PULL-OFF: Place both fingers on the notes to be sounded. Strike the first note and without picking, pull the finger off to sound the second (lower) note.

LEGATO SLIDE: Strike the first note and then slide the same fret-hand finger up or down to the second note. The second note is not struck.

SHIFT SLIDE: Same as legato slide, except the second note is struck.

TRILL: Very rapidly alternate between the notes indicated by continuously hammering on and pulling off.

TAPPING: Hammer ("tap") the fret indicated with the pick-hand index or middle finger and pull off to the note fretted by the fret hand.

NATURAL HARMONIC: Strike the note while the fret-hand lightly touches the string directly over the fret indicated.

PINCH HARMONIC: The note is fretted normally and a harmonic is produced by adding the edge of the thumb or the tip of the index finger of the pick hand to the normal pick attack.

PICK SCRAPE: The edge of the pick is rubbed down (or up) the string, producing a scratchy sound.

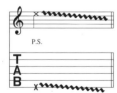

MUFFLED STRINGS: A percussive sound is produced by laying the fret hand across the string(s) without depressing, and striking them with the pick hand.

PALM MUTING: The note is partially muted by the pick hand lightly touching the string(s) just before the bridge.

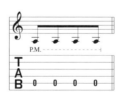

RAKE: Drag the pick across the strings indicated with a single motion.

TREMOLO PICKING: The note is picked as rapidly and continuously as possible.

VIBRATO BAR DIVE AND RETURN: The pitch of the note or chord is dropped a specified number of steps (in rhythm) then returned to the original pitch.

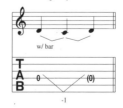

VIBRATO BAR SCOOP: Depress the bar just before striking the note, then quickly release the bar.

VIBRATO BAR DIP: Strike the note and then immediately drop a specified number of steps, then release back to the original pitch.

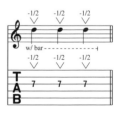

96